FATHERS IN FAITH

FATHERS in FAITH

Reflections on Parenthood and a Christian Life

Allan Hugh Cole Jr.

EDITOR

CASCADE *Books* · Eugene, Oregon

FATHERS IN FAITH
Reflections on Parenthood and a Christian Life

Cascade Books
An Imprint of Wipf and Stock Publishers
199 W. 8th Ave., Suite 3
Eugene, OR 97401

www.wipfandstock.com

ISBN 13: 978-1-61097-069-3

Cataloging-in-Publication data:

    Fathers in faith : reflections on parenthood and a Christian life / edited by Allan Hugh Cole Jr.

    xvi + 100 p.; 23 cm—Includes bibliographical references and index.

    ISBN 13: 978-1-61097-069-3

    1. Fatherhood—Religious aspects—Christianity. 2. Fatherhood—Anecdcotes. 3. Parenting—Religious aspects—Christianity—Anecdotes. I. Cole, Allan Hugh. II. Title.

BV4529.17. F20. 2013

For Allan H. Cole,
faithful father

"Fathers make known to children your faithfulness." —Isaiah 38:19

Contents

Contributors

M. CRAIG BARNES has served as a pastor to four congregations. He is currently President and Professor of Pastoral Ministry and Leadership at Princeton Theological Seminary. He has written seven books, including: *The Pastor as Minor Poet: Texts and Subtexts in the Ministerial Life*; *Searching for Home: Spirituality for Restless Souls*; *An Extravagant Mercy: Reflections on Ordinary Things*; and *Belonging Body and Soul*. He also serves as an editor at large and frequent contributor to the *Christian Century*. He is married to Dawne Hess Barnes. They have three delightful children and a hairy dog named Esau.

DALE BROWN is the founding director of the Buechner Institute and the chairperson of the Department of English at King College in Bristol, Tennessee. For twenty years he was a professor of English at Calvin College in Grand Rapids, Michigan, and there directed the Festival of Faith & Writing. His extensive interviews with more than thirty American writers have appeared in his books *Of Fiction and Faith* and *Conversations with American Writers*. He has also written a critical biography of Frederick Buechner, *The Book of Buechner*. He lives in Bristol, Tennessee, with his wife, Gayle.

RODNEY R. CLAPP is an editor with Wipf and Stock Publishers. He writes regularly for the *Christian Century*, and is the author of more than one hundred articles and seven books, including, *Johnny Cash and the Great American Contradiction: Christianity and the Battle for the Soul of a Nation*; *Families at the Crossroads: Beyond Traditional & Modern Options*; *Tortured Wonders: Christian Spirituality for People, Not Angels*; *Boarder Crossings: Christian Trespasses on Popular Culture and Public Affairs*; and *A Peculiar*

People: The Church as Culture in a Post-Christian Society. He and his wife, Sandy, are parents to Jesselyn.

ALLAN HUGH COLE JR. is academic dean and professor in the Nancy Taylor Williamson Distinguished Chair of Pastoral Care at Austin Presbyterian Theological Seminary, Austin, Texas. He is the author of several books, including, *The Life of Prayer: Mind, Body, and Soul; Good Mourning: Getting through Your Grief; Be Not Anxious: Pastoral Care of Disquieted Souls; The Faith and Friendships of Teenage Boys;* and *Losers, Loners, and Rebels: The Spiritual Struggles of Boys* (both coauthored with Donald Capps and Robert C. Dykstra). He is editor of *A Spiritual Life: Perspectives from Poets, Prophets, and Preachers;* and *From Midterms to Ministry: Practical Theologians on Pastoral Beginnings.* An ordained minister in the Presbyterian Church (USA), he has served congregations in upstate New York and on Long Island. He and his wife, Tracey, are parents to Meredith and Holly.

MARTIN B. COPENHAVER is senior pastor of Wellesley Congregational Church, United Church of Christ, in Wellesley, Massachusetts, where he has served since 1994. He is the author of five books: *Living Faith While Holding Doubts; To Begin at the Beginning: An Introduction to the Christian Faith; Good News in Exile* (coauthored with Anthony B. Robinson and William Willimon); *Words for the Journey: Letters to Our Teenagers about Life and Faith* (coauthored with Anthony B. Robinson); and *This Odd and Wondrous Calling: The Public and Private Lives of Two Ministers* (coauthored with Lillian Daniel). Martin writes for a number of periodicals, including the *Christian Century*, where he also serves as an editor at large. He serves on the Board of Trustees of Andover Newton Theological School, where he also teaches preaching, and on the Board of Advisors of Yale Divinity School. Martin and his wife, Karen, have two adult children, Alanna and Todd.

GREG GARRETT is the father of Jake and Chandler, and, if all goes according to plan, the stepfather of Lily and Sophie. He is the author of over a dozen books, including the novels *Free Bird* and *Shame*; the spiritual autobiographies *Crossing Myself* and *No Idea*; and the theological books *The Other Jesus, Faithful Citizenship,* and *We Get to Carry Each Other: The Gospel according to U2.* He also writes regularly for *Patheos, Huffington Post,* and publications including the *Washington Post, Relevant, Christianity Today,* the

Christian Science Monitor, and *Reform* (UK). He is professor of English at Baylor University, writer in residence at the Seminary of the Southwest, and a licensed lay preacher in the Episcopal Church. He lives in Austin, Texas.

ALBERT Y. HSU is an editor at InterVarsity Press and the author of *Grieving a Suicide*; *The Suburban Christian*; and *Singles at the Crossroads*. He is also a PhD student in educational studies at Trinity Evangelical Divinity School in Deerfield, Illinois, and serves as senior warden on the vestry of Church of the Savior, an Anglican congregation in Wheaton, Illinois. He is married to Ellen Hsu and father to two young boys, Josiah and Elijah.

DAVID H. JENSEN is professor in the Clarence N. and Betty B. Frierson Distinguished Chair of Reformed Theology and Associate Dean for Academic Programs at Austin Presbyterian Theological Seminary, in Austin, Texas. His teaching and research center on the intersection of Christian theology and everyday life. He has written several books, including, *Parenting*; *Living Hope: The Future and Christian Faith*; *Responsive Labor: A Theology of Work*; *Graced Vulnerability: A Theology of Childhood*; *In the Company of Others: A Dialogical Christology*; and an edited volume, *The Lord and Giver of Life: Perspectives on Constructive Pneumatology*. He is married to Molly Hadley Jensen and is a father to a daughter, Grace, and a son, Finn.

ERIK KOLBELL is a UCC minister and licensed psychotherapist. Having previously served as the Minister of Social Justice at New York City's Riverside Church, Erik now ministers largely through his writing. Kolbell's work has covered a wide variety of topics, from the spiritual to the practical, with a common theme being that of tying ethical principles to everyday living. He is the author of numerous books, including *What Jesus Meant: The Beatitudes and a Meaningful Life*; *Were You There?: Finding Ourselves at the Foot of the Cross*; *The God of Second Chances*; and *Lifescripts for Family and Friends: What to Say in 101 of Life's Most Troubling and Uncomfortable Situations*, a guidebook for difficult conversations. He has appeared on the *Today Show* and *Dateline* on NBC, on CBS's the *Early Show*, on the *Charlie Rose Show* on PBS, on *Morning Joe* on MSNBC, on the *Jane Pauley Show*, and *Your Total Health*, on local television, and on numerous radio programs. Erik and his wife, Ann, are parents to Kate.

MICHAEL L. LINDVALL serves as the pastor of the Brick Presbyterian Church in the City of New York. He has previously served as pastor to congregations in Ann Arbor, Michigan, and Northport, Long Island. A writer whose essays, book reviews, sermons, and fiction have appeared in a variety of church-related and secular periodicals, he has authored two novels, *The Good News from North Haven*, and *Leaving North Haven*. He has also written several books of accessible theology: *A Geography of God*; *What Did Jesus Do: A Crash Course on His Life and Times*; and most recently, *Knowing God's Triune Story*. He is married to Terri Vaun Smith. They have three adult children: Madeline, Benjamin, and Grace.

ANTHONY B. ROBINSON is an ordained minister of the United Church of Christ who has served four congregations in the western United States. He is the author of twelve books, including *Transforming Congregational Culture*, and most recently *Called to Lead: I and II Timothy for Today's Pastoral Leaders*, with Robert W. Wall. He contributes regularly to publications such as the *Christian Century*, *Congregations*, and the *Journal for Preachers*. He serves the church as a speaker, teacher, author, and consultant. He is a senior consultant with the Atlanta-based Center for Progressive Renewal, and also leads the Seattle-based ecumenical organization, Congregational Leadership Northwest. Tony lives in Seattle with his wife, Linda Jambor Robinson. These days he enjoys being a grandfather.

Preface

Proverbial wisdom holds that experience is the best teacher. If true, then writing about experience finishes a close second—at least for some of us. For many writers, the act of writing teaches. It helps me explore my experiences, learn from them, and perceive more clearly how they shape who I am and who I want to be. I write because I aspire to know more. I also write in order to heal, which almost always involves learning.

This collection of essays stems from an aspiration to know more about fatherhood and to learn from other fathers. It also relates to one of my foremost realizations since becoming a father—namely, parents need one another. We need one another more than many of us ever imagine before we have children and face the joys, sorrows, successes, failures, opportunities, and challenges that come with parenthood. If it takes a village to raise a child, it takes a trusted band of parents to rear one another.

Not long after our second child was born, my wife, Tracey, and I joined a class—as much a support group—that meets Sunday mornings at our church. Called My Connections, it consists of parents: mostly those with younger children, but a few parents of older children as well. We gather weekly to reflect on and discuss a range of topics and concerns related to parenthood and a Christian life. Members take turns providing leadership for the group, sometimes enlisting outsider expertise and sometimes not. I have learned a great deal from participating in this class. What I have learned has helped me become a more competent and confident father. For this I am grateful.

Even more significant than learning about the various topics related to parenting has been the experiences of support, born of solidarity, that this class has provided. I sense that others in the group feel similarly. On many occasions, when exhausted, confused, or otherwise struggling in my parenting—and on a few days when I felt like an awful father—listening to the stories of others—my mates on the parenting voyage—provided a healing balm for my fatherly soul. Time and again, My Connections has served as a beacon guiding me into calmer parenting waters. The fact that many in this group of parents meet regularly outside the Sunday morning class, and that it has spawned close friendships, indicates its importance to its members.

I take from these experiences that we parents need one another. More than that, we need to risk sharing our experiences. This sharing must include not only joys and successes in raising our children (which most of us find easier to reveal) but also our questions, concerns, mistakes, pain, and hopes. This sharing fosters wisdom, perspective, and a measure of solidarity that buoys parents when they struggle to stay afloat in rough parenting waters. This sharing also provides for more confidence and hope. All of these provisions for parents may serve to benefit the children they love and want the best for in their lives.

This book offers fathers a crew of companions for their own parenting voyage—a different sort of My Connections group. I have invited some of the wisest men I know, all of whom happen to be fathers and from whom I have learned much, to reflect on their experiences of fatherhood and what these have taught them. I believe that you will learn from them as you feel supported and challenged in your own parenting. Each essay stands alone, which means you may feel free to read them in any order.

Nothing has been more important, instructive, or life-giving to me than becoming a father. At the same time, nothing has posed more questions, prompted more anxiety, caused more self-critique, or elicited more appreciation for the opportunity to learn from others than fatherhood. The Apostle Paul wrote to early Christians: "Encourage one another and build up each other, as indeed you are doing" (1 Thessalonians 5:11). A band of trusted fathers who encourage one another and build each other up are gifts from God.

Acknowledgments

I am grateful to the colleagues and friends who contributed to this book. Each of them has taught me about many matters through the years, whether in their writings, in conversation, or both. I appreciate the care with which they approached the subject matter of this book, and also the honesty, compassion, and courage they have demonstrated in these pages, to fathers and to all who care for children.

It has been a pleasure to work with Cascade Books on this project. K. C. Hanson, editor in chief; Christian Amondson, assistant managing editor; their colleagues at Wipf and Stock Publishers, including Heather Carraher, Amelia Reising, and others, model efficiency and professionalism in publishing. I appreciate their support and encouragement.

I am grateful to three people who read my essay for this volume and provided helpful responses. Sheri Reynolds, Greg Garrett, and especially Elizabeth Damewood Gaucher, trusted friends and gifted writers, helped me improve my contribution.

The Austin Presbyterian Theological Seminary community, including faculty, staff, and students; our Board of Trustees; and our alumni/ae make serving in theological education my privilege and joy. I am particularly grateful to Alison Riemersma, my assistant, for her generous spirit and consistent support.

My wife, Tracey, and our daughters, Meredith and Holly, continue to touch my life in ways that show forth the grace of God. Nothing makes me happier than sharing life with them.

My parents, Allan and Jeri Cole, have demonstrated through their own faithful parenting that parental love sits next to Godly love on the bench of life.

This book is dedicated to my father, Allan H. Cole. Consistently faithful, he enriches my life beyond words.

1

Decisions, Decisions:
A Hesitant Approach to Fatherhood

ALLAN HUGH COLE JR.

Maybe, Maybe Not

It's early. The four of us lie in bed—in the *same* bed. Our daughters, ages six and four, still end up in their parents' bed sometimes, especially when it storms. It rained hard all night, a rarity in central Texas. Thunder rolled in from the hill country to the west. Lightning flashed around us, lining the sky with strobe-like bursts. A steady wind blew for hours, making our 1938 windows flex and pop.

It's quiet now. I'm the only one awake. I think of the bluebonnets enjoying the cascade of water.

I share a king-size pillow with two little girls, our heads sandwiched together. Mine lies in the middle. Soft brown hair, Meredith's straight and Holly's curly, touches my ears and neck. One strand tickles me just below my right jawline.

Both girls still smell of lavender-scented shampoo and bodywash, lingering from when they took a bath together the night before. I know they won't do that much longer, and I will miss it. Experiencing sheer joy means missing it when it's gone. I will miss the Santa-Claus beards they form with bubble bath as they giggle and say, "Look, Daddy!" I will miss their creativity with household items that become makeshift bath toys. I will miss taking part in the array of imaginative games spawned by being in the tub. I will miss too the kind of childhood freedom that a bath provides, freedom that a father also may join. And I'll miss that lavender scent. It brings me back to their earliest days of life. It reminds me of how these two forever changed *my* life.

I turn my head to the right. Peering over one of my girls I see Tracey, my wife of twenty years. A soft blue sheet pulled to her neck outlines a petite, olive-skinned body barely visible in the dark. Her hands about six inches apart, the first two knuckles on each one hangs over the sheet. She grasps it while sleeping on her side. As she faces us, her chin tilts upward, as if she's prepared to take in the scene too.

Tracey is beautiful, graceful, smart, and funny. I view her in several ways: as my partner, lover, confidant, fellow dreamer, and friend. But perhaps most meaningful to me in this season of our shared life, she's "Momma" to Meredith and Holly, and the rudder for family life. Our girls adore her. I adore her too.

The deep and rhythmic breathing of "my three ladies," as I refer to them, faint yet audible in the foreground of steady rain, sounds melodic. I'm at home with the loves of my life. Though storms have raged around us throughout the night, they have brought us together, and I feel at peace. More than that, I experience deep joy and contentment—as in, "Thank you, God. There's no place I'd rather be, now or ever." It seems impossible that I was hesitant about becoming a father. But I was.

Understanding My Hesitance

Tracey and I were married thirteen years when Meredith was born. We put off the question of having children as long as we could. The biological clock forced us to decide. Numerous friends who married after we did started their families a few years into their marriages. As their kids aged, several of these friends began to inquire about our plans for parenthood, sometimes subtly and sometimes not. "You two have been married for a long time. What are you waiting for?" some would ask. "It's the best thing, ever! You don't know what you're missing," a few said about parenthood. Even more pointed, a former parishioner once said to me in a matter-of-fact tone: "You are being unfaithful if you are able to have children and choose not to." That last comment was inexcusable, but inquiries into our plans for having children were somewhat common, among friends and acquaintances alike. We were married, so we should have children, the logic seemed to go. The longer we were married without children, the more the curiosity—and in some cases, the disapproval—seemed to increase.

Interesting was that though eager for us to become parents, our families rarely broached the subject. We appreciated their restraint. An exception that comes to mind occurred on our tenth wedding anniversary, when Tracey's ninety-three-year-old grandmother said to me after she raised the question of our having children, "Allan, it's been long enough. Plant the seed!" In a separate conversation, she noted "If you want a boy, leave your boots on."

I own several pairs of boots, and I'm proud of them, but I tend to take them off at the front door.

Inquiries into our plans for parenthood made me uncomfortable. On the one hand, these queries felt intrusive. We never asked these kinds of personal questions of our friends or of anyone else for that matter. We knew of people who wanted children and who tried to conceive without success. Their disappointment and grief served to caution us on the rare occasion when we considered asking about others' plans for parenthood. It's a sensitive matter for some couples, for different reasons. Tracey and I operated with the assumption that people would share what they wanted to share about their plans for children, if and when they wanted to, without our asking. Propriety and politeness called for restraint.

On the other hand, and more discomforting for me, questions about our plans for children made me acknowledge my ambivalence about parenthood and, eventually, compelled me to try to understand it. I found this process of understanding difficult and painful. After all, I could imagine parenthood, especially with Tracey. I could envision the joy it brings and had observed this joy in others. Philosophically, I was "child-centered" for goodness sakes! Yet I remained hesitant about taking my own step into parenthood.

I also assumed that my uncertainty was something of which to be ashamed, especially in light of the eagerness of friends—and seemingly everyone else—to have children, *and* their eagerness for us to have children too. "What's wrong with you?" I'd ask myself, even as I imagined others wanting to ask that question of me. Consequently, I tended to respond to the queries about Tracey and me having children by changing the subject, or by saying something to the effect of "We're not ready" or, in a playful tone, "We're working on it!" Sometimes, I ignored the questions altogether.

It turns out that my hesitancy with fatherhood had less to do with children and more to do with me. This hesitancy turned around three matters: first, a lack of experience with children, and a corresponding dearth of confidence relating to children; second, a concern that having children would bring an unwanted change in my marriage and lifestyle; and, most significant, a fear that I would not meet the responsibilities of parenting sufficiently, which would prevent my children from thriving. I will comment on each of these factors relating to my hesitancy.

I had little experience with children. I also lacked confidence in my ability to interact with them, relate to them, and care for them. This lack of confidence stemmed from lack of experience. As a newly ordained minister at the age of twenty-six and serving my first congregation, I recall vividly my awareness that the most interaction I had ever had with young children was when I offered children's sermons on Sunday mornings. I simply had not been around children very often.

Likewise, the thought of caring for children made me anxious, especially when I focused on the responsibility that comes with appropriate caring. Although I viewed myself as a nurturing and responsible person— a former colleague once called me hyperresponsible—I felt the weight of *parenting* responsibilities. I now wonder whether the weight of being a very young pastor, which, for me, brought its own burdens related to responsibility, figured in to my resistance to parenthood. Whether it did or not, the prospects of parenting scared me. At the same time, I assumed that others, meaning those who became parents, were immune to these feelings of apprehension. This assumption added to my internal struggle, making me feel even more out of step with my peers.

I've since discovered the inaccuracy of my assumption. Many parents I talk to recount feeling uneasy and lacking confidence when embarking on parenthood. Perhaps apprehensiveness is more the rule than the exception. But I did not know this when Tracey and I began thinking about having children, and almost no one who *was* having children admitted to his or her own ambivalence or concerns. Accordingly, I assumed if one felt the way I did—apprehensive, lacking in confidence, ambivalent—then one was not ready to be a parent. So I kept putting off the decision.

At the same time, married life was rich and full already. I didn't want that to change. I've known couples who, if their children were planned, seemed to start a family, either because they were "supposed to," or because they lacked something in their marriages. As regards the latter, they might not put it this way themselves but they revealed a working assumption that having a child would enrich them as couples and help make their marriages better. Children can indeed enrich a marriage and often do. My girls have enriched my marriage in untold ways, far beyond what I ever imagined possible before they were born. My girls have enriched every aspect of my life. But my experience has been that couples who lack something in their relationship before having children—intimacy, wholeness, pleasure, purpose, or other significant qualities of couplehood—rarely have their needs met simply by having children. In fact, experience has shown me that children often place greater strain on a marriage, especially unfulfilled ones. After all, though wonderfully satisfying and even exhilarating—"the best thing ever"—parenting is also difficult, demanding, challenging, exhausting and, at times, terrifying.

Tracey and I were content. We spent the first nine years of our marriage completing graduate studies. We moved from North Carolina to New Jersey to New York, back to New Jersey, and then back to New York. After I finished school, we moved to Austin, Texas, where we still live. Finally able to settle for a bit, both of us were thriving in our respective careers in Austin—Tracey as a geriatric social worker, I as a professor. We were happy. We enjoyed our work. We appreciated our freedom. We prized the ability to be spontaneous and unconventional in our routines. We had a dog! We had sufficient money. We liked spending time with friends and with each other. We also appreciated solitude. Life was good.

I assumed that having children would mean giving up many of these pleasures.

As I think back, I realize that Tracey felt a measure of reticence over having children and for some of the same reasons, especially in the first years of our marriage. However, she was less hesitant than I was after that time. She began wanting to have children, even though she maintained a measure of apprehension. My hesitance persisted. I continued to imagine parenthood more in terms of what one had to give up rather than of what one would gain.

But that was only a part of what led to my putting off parenthood. As I have noted, my hesitance related far more to my fear of being a father, and especially of the responsibilities of fatherhood, than to what I envisioned having to give up. I think I recognized that while parenthood requires that one give up some of the freedoms, pleasures, and opportunities one enjoys prior to having children (or at least to postpone them), one also gains new forms of these when having children. I welcomed experiencing new kinds of freedom, pleasure, and opportunity that children provide. I assumed these would inform some of the many gifts that parenthood offers. I'd witnessed friends receiving these gifts themselves. My hesitance to become a father persisted, nonetheless; and this stemmed from a deep fear that my inadequacies as a person, and therefore as a parent, would cause my children pain, perhaps for life. When considering fatherhood I inevitably focused more on resources that I perceived I lacked, and less on those I reckoned I possessed.

From Hesitance to Unsurpassed Joy and Gratitude

What squelched my hesitancy about fatherhood was Tracey becoming pregnant with Meredith. The hesitancy seemed to dissolve with a positive home-pregnancy test. Now I was exhilarated . . . and terrified. With regard to the terror, I remember vividly my eyes popping open in the wee hours of the next morning, around 2:00 a.m. Adrenaline pumped through me and my first thought was, "I need to buy more life insurance!" But I also recall, just as clearly, a kind and degree of joy and excitement about the future that I'd never known. I experienced it again when we found out that Tracey was pregnant with Holly. It was the same way I felt six years later, again in the early morning hours, as I lay in bed with my family after the storm: "Thank you, God. There's no place I'd rather be, now or ever."

All the joy and elation joined to fatherhood notwithstanding, becoming the father I desire to be has required work—a lot of work. That's what I want to comment on in the rest of this essay. By work I mean internal and relational along with spiritual soul-searching. Though no longer hesitant about fatherhood, I am still afraid some of the time; and my fears, related to the responsibilities of parenting and my own perceived shortcomings, can and do get in the way of my being who and what I want to be, for my girls, Tracey, and myself.

Exploring my strengths along with my imperfections and fears, and also finding the courage to acknowledge them, to myself and others, has helped to lessen the persistence and power of my fears. Pain has power over us but more so with unacknowledged pain. At the same time, becoming a better father has required me to function less attuned to my imperfections, less beholden to my fears, and more attuned to the gift and delight of children and of a parenting life.

I now want to note what has encouraged my functioning in these ways, on what has grounded some of my work to become a better father. Several discoveries have helped me attune to and celebrate the delight that joins with parenthood, even amid the challenges. That delight can be breathtaking. Of course, I have discovered much more than I can include here. With parenting comes ongoing discovery. But I want share a few of the discoveries that have enriched my parenting life.

Many of these discoveries have come by way of my children. This fact reminds me of the proverbial wisdom that children teach their parents. Just as many of these discoveries link to my faith. In particular, the wisdom of certain biblical texts and a commitment to seeking to live accordingly have shaped how I think and act as a father. This wisdom, though never a panacea, buoys me by keeping me mindful of what and who sustains me as a father. In turn, this wisdom provides guidance and confidence for reaching my goal of parenting with more confidence and calm.

The Gift of the Moment

This is the day that the Lord has made;
let us rejoice and be glad in it. —Psalms 118:24

I have known this passage from the Psalms for many years. I believe I first heard it as a young child, around age four or five, at the Holy Cross Episcopal Church in Simpsonville, South Carolina. It's one of those passages that reach way back for me. It speaks to me "a word from the Lord."

While serving as a pastor I proclaimed these words more times than I can now recall when beginning worship services. People of God rightly remind themselves of these words, in worship and in daily life. We worship a gift-giving God whose supreme gift is the offer of each new day. Every day, every moment of every day, is freely given by the One who provides. People of faith across a variety of religious traditions affirm this belief. We affirm that life issues from God.

For Christians, Jesus's words prove instructive: "I came that they may have life, and have it abundantly" (John 10:10). When we lack awareness of this divine gift of life abundant, or when we otherwise diminish it, we forego the opportunity to savor its power, opportunity, beauty, and grace. Keep in mind the fleeting nature of life, for all of us. We begin dying the moment we enter the world. Some people die sooner than we want or think is fair, but eventually everyone dies. Consequently, every day—every moment of life—matters. Jesus points to God's desire for us, to have abundant life.

Despite my proclamation of the psalmist's words, and also my appreciation for them, I have not lived by them. I have not allowed what they say on behalf of God, "the Lord and giver of life,"[1] to ground my way of being in the world. In fact, often I have struggled to find satisfaction with living for the day. I have struggled to recognize, not to mention rejoice in, the gift of each life moment.

I have found it much easier to look ahead in anticipation of what comes next—in anticipation of tomorrow. This inclination, part DNA and part self-imposed, relates especially to my vocational life, one centered, ironically, in following Jesus—the one who said "Do not worry about tomorrow" (Matthew 6:34)—and on helping to form and educate others who do the same. As a scholar and administrator, I tend to anticipate, if not worry about, the next book to write, the next course to teach, the next professional focus or opportunity, the next grant initiative for my school, the next faculty promotion or hire, the next operating budget, the next plan to reach the next goal. In doing so, I sometimes neglect the joy, satisfaction, challenges, and growth spawned by present vocational rewards or experiences.

I regret that this inclination has also touched my parenting. Too often I have been pulled away from the richness—the gift—of the present moment with my children by thoughts of their futures. These thoughts relate to their happiness, well-being, and safety; and to providing for their education, activities, friendships, religious formation, physical and material needs, and even their inheritance. Concerns for the future relate to the weighty responsibilities of fatherhood, for me a carryover from preparenthood days. Sometimes these concerns leach in to contaminate the appropriately carefree moments of life in the present, the gift shared between parent and child, what, as the psalmist recognizes, "the Lord has made."

I've written elsewhere about a kind of restlessness that, again instructed by the psalmist (Psalms 42:5), I call the "disquieted soul."[2] This restlessness gives rise to a tendency to look ahead, to push forward, to drive toward tomorrow, to begin working for what comes next, to shore up the future for oneself or one's children, and to live anxiously. This restlessness

---

1. The Nicene Creed, among the earliest professions of faith, contains this phrase to describe qualities of the Holy Spirit.

2. Cole, *Be Not Anxious: Pastoral Care of Disquieted Souls.*

conceals the benefits of the here and now and curbs rejoicing and gladness in the day. This restlessness prevents one from embracing the gifts of life and parenting in their fullness. Words of the first-century Roman philosopher Seneca describe my experience: "They lose the day in expectation of the night, and the night in fear of the dawn."[3]

I have pondered the psalmist's words for decades. I hear and understand their significance—and their grace—afresh since becoming a father. Parenthood has challenged me to live more attuned to these words. Their echo in the midst of daily family life offers a gentle but sure corrective. They restrain my tendency to look ahead unnecessarily or excessively, to have one eye focused on the horizon when the present vistas call for my full attention. Paraphrasing wisdom attributed to Seneca, the psalmist's words remind me that anticipating tomorrow risks losing today.

My children have helped me embrace the biblical wisdom of living for today. Like all young children, they live for the moment. They give little if any attention to much else. I've noticed with my girls that even when something special awaits them beyond the present moment—a visit with grandparents, going to their favorite toystore, swimming with beloved friends, creating art, watching a video—their energy remains attached to what they are currently engaged in, thinking about, working on, or enjoying. What may come next does not crowd out what's before them.

Here is an illustration. Not long ago, Holly, my four-year-old, was playing with one of her dolls. Captivated by the conversation she imagined between herself and the doll, she had constructed a rather intricate dialogue between them. It included offers of praise, a question or two, a mild disagreement, and vivid language about what they were doing together. Viewing all this, I was reminded of G. K. Chesterton's wisdom—namely that "it might reasonably be maintained that the true object of all human life is play."[4] If so, the psalmist might well have put it this way: "This is the day that the Lord has made; let us rejoice, be glad, and *play* in it." It was enchanting to watch my daughter so glad and so free in her play.

When she paused for a moment I must have assumed that she was bored or "stuck"; and, ever the one to look ahead, I asked "What do you want to do now, honey?" She looked at me rather sternly, with a furrowed brow and hands on her hips, and said, "Dad, can't you see I'm playing?" Fair enough. Lesson learned.

3. Seneca, "On the Shortness of Life," 341.
4. Chesterton, *All Things Considered*, 96.

Sure, a concern for my children's future needs, desires, and well-being remains; but allowing that concern to sit front and center in my line of vision impairs my front-row view of their lives being lived *now*. The psalmist's words temper my tendency to miss seeing and experiencing the fullness of shared life—the sacred gift of parenthood—unwrapping before me *today*. And today is all that we have.

My children teach me daily the value of the psalmist's wisdom as they model how to embrace it.

The Gift of Faithfulness and Integrity

You will know them by their fruits. —*Matthew 7:16*

Parenthood also has taught me the necessity of my own modeling. I must act in ways congruent with what I tell Meredith and Holly is important, moral, ethical, just, faithful, or otherwise appropriate. Just as I learn from what my children do, they learn from what I do. They learn from what I do more than from what I say. Children know their parents by the fruit they bear, by what they exhibit in their daily lives. Parents thus need to *exemplify* the qualities of relationship, values, and behaviors they want their children to associate with them, and that they want their children to adopt. Merely speaking of these or extolling their merits does not suffice. In point of fact, as others in this volume will also note, when what parents say and do lacks congruency or consistency, they send their kids a confusing message: "Do as I say, not as I do." Children hear in this: "What I (their father) say is not important enough for me to do it, and therefore isn't really important enough for you (my children) to do it, either." Upon considering this message, we recognize its hypocrisy and futility. But we communicate this message more often than we may realize.

Here are some ways that I communicate this message. I tout the importance of consistency in keeping one's word or in meeting one's obligations and I prove inconsistent myself. I have in mind occasions when I waver on a particular commitment I've made to our girls because I'm tired after a long day, such as taking them to the park before supper or joining them in the pool, when I have said to them time and again that I expect them *not* to waver on their commitments, such as completing homework or household chores before going out to play. In a similar fashion, I speak to our children about the virtues of reading more and spending less time on the computer or watching television ("screen time," as we call it) as I scroll on my phone looking at new e-mails or surf the Internet on my iPad. Another example: I tell our kids that material possessions do not make a person happy and that our family has so much more than most families in the world. Then I continue to buy and consume less discriminately and more excessively than I should, for them and for Tracey and myself, and they witness my actions.

Another example is when I laud the virtues of my girls speaking in kind voices when frustrated with one another; and in *my* moment of frustration, with them or with someone else, I speak more harshly than I should. In each of these cases my actions do not square with my words. I find it easy to tell my kids what I want for them and expect from them. I find it more difficult to remain consistent in modeling these said desires and expectations myself.

Let me be clear. I'm not suggesting that any of these inconsistencies I've mentioned makes for an unpardonable parenting sin. All parents have finer and less fine moments interacting with their children and setting the example they want their children to follow. Moreover, parents expressing anger, frustration, or disappointment in appropriate ways (firmly but not harshly) may give children confidence in expressing their own emotions as opposed to holding on to them or denying true feelings. Unexpressed feelings may become harmful over time. My point is that when I make the parenting mistake of asking my kids to "Do as I say, not as I do," I need quickly to remember the ineffectiveness of this approach, not to mention the injustice of it, and seek to do better. This approach confuses my girls and does little to nothing for helping garner what Tracey and I want for them. Actions speak louder than words, but my words and actions must correspond for my children to understand and embrace them.

I'm naming here a need for parental integrity. All people should strive for integrity in their lives, whether parents or not. For people who follow Jesus, faithfulness *requires* integrity. Yet fatherhood has made me strive even harder to maintain my integrity with what I say and do, because more is at stake than ever before. Two sets of delicious brown eyes watch me. Meredith and Holly pay close attention to my words and behaviors; and they assess the degree to which I maintain consistency between them. They observe me and learn from me—constantly. As the psychologist C. G. Jung observed, "Children are educated by what the grown-up *is* and not by his talk."[5]

5. Jung, *Psychological Reflections*, 111.

I did not understand the magnitude of this phenomenon before having children. Parenting has helped me keep this wisdom in the forefront of my mind; to gauge what and who I am with greater depth and interest than ever before because doing so helps me model—and teach—what I want my children to value and exemplify. In a similar vein, parenthood has prodded me to remember the close relationship between what I do and who my children perceive me to be. Although I am an introspective person by nature, having children leads me to consider more intentionally how what I do informs who I am, on the one hand, and how my children view me by virtue of what I do, on the other. In other words, I'm aware that in the presence of my children, what I say and how I say it, the manner in which I say people should be treated and how I treat them, the degree to which I remain true to my word, the activities that garner my time and interest—all of this and more shapes how my daughters see me and, in turn, how they see themselves. They do as they see me do. They value what they see me value as indicated by what I do. Perhaps the prophet Isaiah had this relationship in mind when he spoke these words: "Fathers make known to children your faithfulness" (Isaiah 38:19).

My attempt at modeling what I want for my children plays out in various ways, some of which I anticipated before becoming a parent and some of which I did not. But never have I paid closer attention to my *language*. I monitor the words I use and how I use them with more energy than ever before. I'll share some examples.

In keeping with their inclinations, my girls were resisting going to bed one evening. As they kept giggling, tossing stuffed animals at one another, and engaging in other behaviors that amused them and irritated me, I said to them, as my frustration boiled over, "Stop playing 'grab ass' and get in bed!" In case you're not familiar with this expression, "playing grab ass" is Southern for "horsing around." Of course, telling my girls to stop playing "grab ass" only prolonged the bedtime ritual. It did nothing to encourage their focus on going to sleep. Now I had to explain to them what "grab ass" meant.

I don't recall my exact explanation. I remember explaining that "ass" is another word for "butt," which, of course, they knew. I also stressed that I wish I had asked them to stop playing "grab butt," adding that sometimes grownups say "ass" when they more appropriately should say "butt." Every time I uttered the word "butt," their giggles got louder. I was thankful that Tracey was not present.

I should have said, "Stop horsing around" instead of bringing anatomy into the conversation. With little girls, talking about anatomy ranks up there with talking about bodily functions and Hello Kitty. Finding pleasure in bathroom talk and having anatomical preoccupations typically gets credited to little boys, not to mention men, but I've learned that little girls seem equally interested in these matters and, apparently, just as willing to discuss them.

Getting back to my "grab ass" remark, I had to think on my feet; and, in the heat of my frustration, with two sets of eager brown eyes staring, I came up with my best explanation for uttering it. Granted, it wasn't my best save as a father. I've had better ones. But even when seeing the puzzled looks on my children's faces I assumed I'd smoothed things over well enough.

Not long after this event we had one of their friends over to play, a sweet little five-year-old girl. While the three of them were in our daughter's bedroom, I overheard one of my daughters say to this friend, matter of fact, "My dad doesn't want us playing grab ass!" My other daughter immediately added, "Yeah. No grab ass!" After a moment of silence, the five-year-old friend responded, "Grab what?" At this point, I walked to the other side of the house.

Many parents have had the experience of hearing their child utter an inappropriate word or phrase, unfailingly in the presence of those beyond the family circle, which they overheard a parent saying. I pay closer attention to what I say now that I'm a father, particularly when it's unsuitable for children.

Parenting has led me to pay attention to my language in additional ways. These hold even more significance than refraining from using profanity. I have in mind gossip and critical or unkind talk about others. I don't think I'm prone to this kind of talk, nor do I engage in it routinely. When I do, I regret it and usually feel as though I need a shower. Even so, I am now more apt to catch myself when I veer down a conversational road that I don't want my girls to follow. I want and need to model what I desire for them—what I want them to embrace and exemplify. It sends a confusing message to my children if I correct them when they gossip or speak unkindly about a friend or schoolmate when I speak unkindly about people myself. I'm also now more aware of when other adults engage in this kind of conversation, and I try hard to avoid it, particularly when in earshot of children.

For similar reasons parenting has lessened my propensity to dwell on the negative in my speech. Rather than focusing on the unfavorable, gloomy, or deficient aspects of situations, experiences, or people, which models a particular set of perspectives for my children, I try to stress a positive and hopeful focus and response. I don't deny what may be lacking, nor do I avoid naming the undesirable; but dwelling on it serves little if any positive effect, for parenting or for life.

The writer of Proverbs held that "even children make themselves known by their acts" (Proverbs 20:11). As Jesus put it, "You will know them by their fruits."

Six Years Later

Approaching my seventh year as a parent I better understand my fears and strengths as a father. Though I'm still aware of my need for improvement, I have gained confidence in my parenting abilities. Not surprising, there's nothing I would trade for the privilege of fatherhood. Nothing causes me to feel more gratitude or to experience greater joy or fulfillment. It's hard sometimes. It's tiring, physically and emotionally. With it comes uncertainty and worry about the future. But as was suggested to me years ago, fatherhood has indeed been "the best thing ever!" Some days I am still afraid, but I'm no longer hesitant. Moreover, my fear has less power over me, and I live with it more constructively. At the same time, I remain aware that my fears can still get in the way of my being the father I want to be, and the father I believe God wants me to be.

A couple of years ago, when she was four, Meredith said to me rather prophetically, "Dad, you're not perfect; you're a parent!" Wise beyond her years, she has enlightened me more times than I can count. I later realized that she'd heard this particular statement on a children's television network. She's was right, of course; and I have drawn encouragement from this wisdom that Meredith shared.

From one point of view, with parenthood the stakes are always high. Consequently, parents do well both to embrace the deep responsibilities that come with parenting *and* to know their own limitations while seeking to compensate for them. Gaining more knowledge concerning these responsibilities and limitations informs the necessary and ongoing personal and relational work of parenting and of life.

Then again, parents are not perfect. Those who assume they should be perfect, and those who function overly attuned to their limitations, may worry excessively about how they affect their children. This worry, which may cause one to overthink parenting, does neither the parent nor the child any good. It gets in the way of the abundance joined to the parenting life. One should be attentive to one's parenting, but not overly attentive. Too much focus on one's parenting eventually results in diminishing returns.

I have not sought in this essay to give advice. Most offers of advice, though perhaps well intentioned, prove unhelpful if not also presumptuous. Besides, I knew more about parenting *before* I became a parent! Or, more accurately, I thought I did. In point of fact, parenting always calls for more than a one-size-fits-all approach. Children and parents alike will always be unique persons with differing personalities, strengths, weaknesses, needs, and resources. The best approach to parenting for me might not work as well for you. Why not? Because we differ, and so do our children. Still, I hope that my experience as a father will resonate with the experiences of other parents, particularly fathers, in ways that prove helpful. I hope, too, that by sharing some of my discoveries about fatherhood, including my struggles and shortcomings, others may ponder their own discoveries anew and that these discoveries will enrich their parenting.

The sunshine begins to push through our bedroom blinds. Usually the one to wake first, Holly begins to stir. She flips to the right and then quickly back to the left. She opens her eyes to meet mine. I smile, but also bring my left forefinger to my lips and quietly offer a "Shhhh." She smiles back at me, pauses for a moment, and then, in a tender whisper, says:

"Hi Daddy."

"Hi, Sweetie. How did you sleep?"

"Good, Daddy. How did you sleep?"

"Fine, thank you. Just fine."

"Daddy . . ."

"Yes?"

"I'm ready to start our day."

"Me too, Love. Me too!"

2

Fatherhood as Mystery

DAVID H. JENSEN

The Christian church has often struggled with fathers' roles throughout its history, even though the image of the Father is foundational in the tradition. In Scripture, Father is a primary metaphor for God, present in the Hebrew Bible (e.g., Deut 32:6, "Is not he your father, who created you, who made you and established you?"), and especially pervasive in the New Testament. Jesus's father-language for God has been particularly influential: it is his primary way of referring to God in the Gospels, and it has become, no doubt, the most common name for God in the churches. The most frequently recited prayer in Christian worship (which, tradition has it, Jesus taught the disciples) begins with a simple petition: "Our Father." Many of the churches, moreover, refer to their clergy as "father." This near ubiquity of father language means, in many respects, that there is no way around the Father in Christian Scripture, language, and practice.

Any language employed this frequently has positive and negative consequences. On the one hand, father language for God indicates an intimacy of relation that few words can express: God is the Father who cares for his children, who longs for their flourishing, and who welcomes them home in the fullness of time. On the other hand, the image has contributed to inordinate male authority while it has marginalized women and their leadership gifts throughout the church's history. Too often, Father has become the *only* image for God in the tradition, and we have reaped its consequences. In Mary Daly's trenchant, if hyperbolic, observation: "If God is male, then the male is God."[1] But even when critics argue against the use of father-language in theology and liturgy, the image can become even more conspicuous as an absent Father, unacknowledged and unnamed.

Because the Father appears so often in the church's proclamation, one might expect that theologians would refer frequently to the human experience of fathering. If God is the Father who cares for his children, does this not have consequences for how human fathers understand their own vocation as parents? Sometimes the connections have been drawn. The Bible, of course, has several memorable—and even tender—depictions of fathers and children. Genesis, for example, comprises a long string of family stories, where fathers occupy prominent roles. Many of them are unforgettable, such as Isaac's accidental blessing of his son Jacob (after Jacob deceives him), and his subsequent inability to confer a blessing upon his firstborn, Esau (Genesis 27). Perhaps the most memorable depiction of a father in the New Testament occurs in Jesus's parable of the Prodigal Son (Luke 15:11–32), with its striking narration of a father's generosity and forgiveness upon welcoming home a lost son. But these depictions of fathers and children in Scripture, like most, tend to focus on older or adult children. Rarely in the Bible do we encounter fathers with young children.

Perhaps this relative absence of fathers engaged in acts of child care has resulted in a similar paucity of theological reflection on fatherhood. (The scriptural narratives, no doubt, are products of their time. Only relatively recently in history have fathers also been charged with the ordinary work of child care that have typically been construed as "women's work.") When (male) theologians have mentioned child care in their writing, they stand out as surprising and anomalous. Reformer Martin Luther, for example, reflected on a father's work of diaper-changing as a sacred calling, probably the only time in the church's history that diaper duty has received such lofty praise! Congregationalist pastor Horace Bushnell exhorted fathers in his watershed book on religious education, *Christian Nurture*, to play with their children. But these reflections are exceptional. Even the Holy Family appears odd in the amount of theological attention granted the mother in comparison to the father. Where Mary captures theological attention as the preeminent mother (and saintly person receptive to God's call), Joseph slides into the background, acknowledged but not fully present. Even in Jesus's family there is little material for contemporary fathers to draw upon.

1. Daly, *Beyond God the Father*, 19.

As twenty-first-century fathers in North America continue to take up more of the routine acts of childcare, they need images and concepts about fathering that are resonant with Christian faith and their experiences as caregivers. One place that I have found helpful in exploring a fuller interpretation of fatherhood is to consider the experience of fatherhood as *mystery*, drawing upon the classic Christian understanding of God's nature and relationship with humanity as ultimate mystery. As fathers welcome children into the world, journey with their children, and instruct and discipline children, we are invited into deeper mysteries of faith and being human. This sense of holy mystery, moreover, can sustain fathers in their ordinary acts of caregiving and reminds us that fathering is a sacred vocation. In what follows, I reflect on three mundane mysteries in my own experience as a father and connect them to the Christian affirmation of God as mystery who reveals God's self in relation to others.

Children come into the world as mystery. My wife, Molly, and I are parents of two children: Grace and Finn. Neither of them came into the world "according to plan." Grace came into our lives as an unexpected gift while we were living in a tiny apartment, slogging through graduate school on borrowed money, a couple of part-time jobs, and many dreams for the future. As we were preparing for our dissertations and qualifying exams, we found ourselves completely unprepared for parenting. But as we began to make room in our lives for the child who was coming, we also found ourselves surrounded by others who helped us prepare for the adventure: our own parents, to be sure, but also the fellow members of our church in Nashville. The previous year, Molly and I had taught the confirmation class for the seventh-grade youth. The parents of those teens, as soon as they found out we were expecting a baby, organized a shower for us. Because of that shower, our little apartment accumulated the small necessities of caring for an infant. Were it not for those youth and their parents, we wouldn't have had blankets, clothes, or a car seat for Grace. A book that one of them gave us remains the one book on parenting that I have actually read in all the years since. Those church members helped us welcome the gift that was Grace. When Grace was baptized, the confirmation class stood as her sponsors as she was welcomed into the church. Looking back on it all, I don't know why any of it happened in the way it did: two unprepared graduate students, others in the church who saw a need in two of their members. *When* children come into our lives, and *how* they come into our lives is surrounded by mystery. Parents don't deserve their children, but when they find the room to welcome the mystery that is a child's life, they are forever changed.

Finn came into our lives several years later. After a long period of trial-and-error in parenting, after Grace outgrew diapers, learned to walk, and eventually learned to read, Molly and I decided to have another child. But if Grace came into the world suddenly, Finn came into the world after years of waiting and after hopes that were extinguished almost as soon as they appeared. Finn didn't come into the world according to schedule. We weren't expecting Finn to come into our lives in the way he did, either. The hows and whys of his birth, for me, are still mysterious. I expect this is the case for many parents, whether they experience the birth of a biological child or welcome the long-awaited arrival of an adopted child. Either way, children come into parents' lives as mysterious gifts, surprising us with their sheer otherness, their immediate capacity to change our lives in such dramatic fashion. Grace woke up five times a night for months on end; Finn was fussy; Grace giggled as she sat in her bouncy seat; Finn made us laugh as he chewed on his socks. They changed every day, and so did we. Theologian Rodney Clapp has written of the uniqueness of each child, and how parents experience that uniqueness in disruptive ways: "Every child, from the first midnight it bawls for a feeding to the first bizarre teenage hairstyle, often acts in ways that surprise and even distress parents."[2] Grace and Finn came into our lives on the day we welcomed them into the world, but they also come into our lives anew every day that we share with them. I don't know why it all happened in the way that it did; I don't know what tomorrow holds as I continue to be a father. But when I'm open to the mystery of my children's continual arrival, I am opened to new, even unimagined possibilities in the life that unfolds before me as a father.

Children's worlds are also mysterious to fathers. For me, this is true despite the fact that I have now spent thirteen years with Grace and about half as much time with Finn. Increased familiarity does not diminish mystery. Oftentimes, it seems like we inhabit different worlds. Clapp reflects on this phenomenon as well, by considering the essential "strangeness" of children. He writes, *"Christians have children so we can become the kind of people who welcome strangers."*[3] Children, because they are different from their parents, introduce strange new ways of being and responding in the world. But as parents and children learn to live with each other in their

2. Clapp, *Families at the Crossroads*, 142.
3. Ibid., 138.

mutual strangeness, they become better able to practice the hospitality that is integral to Christian faith. The long-term patterns of care and living together with children can, at their best, make fathers more capable of receiving others into our lives.

I often think differently from my children and routinely act differently. The things that are most important in their lives often seem trivial to mine (and the same goes for their view of my world). I confess that an adolescent girl's world is often more than I can fathom: the relational intensity of her friends, what seems to be the rapid "unfriending" in her social sphere, the frequent texting, the singing of Broadway show tunes and pop hits from *Glee* that can erupt at all hours of the day. There are emotional highs and occasional lows, meltdowns and calm evenings, and at times they seem precipitated by the same events. Sometimes I'm tempted to give up trying to understand. But when I listen to Grace, when we talk about the things that matter most to her, the feelings that are most pressing, I am invited into that world, and she into mine. Many times in the midst of these conversations we begin to understand each others' worlds better, but sometimes we don't. Yet even when we don't, we continue to share our worlds with each other. One of the ways that theologians have understood what it means for human beings to live in God's image is in their capacity to share themselves with others. To be a creature in God's image is to *be with*. Parenting, if nothing else, teaches fathers that we are not alone in God's world, that this mystery of being-with is part of what makes us truly human.

Finn's world, upon first glance, seems more similar to mine. I'm more familiar with the copious characters that populate it: some from movies that I relish (like *Star Wars*), others from his raw imagination. He unravels these elaborate worlds of the imagination with paper and Crayola marker: spaceships and desert animals; undersea cities and robots; family and friends. I enjoy watching him create and give life to these worlds as he draws. It reminds me of the games I played as a kid and my own adventures in imagination. But he is also fascinated with things that I've never heard of, and he gets upset and elated over things that I can scarcely comprehend. His capacity to invent backyard games with balls and sticks is more than I can muster. But as I observe Finn, and even more directly, as I draw or play with him and we act out these characters, I am also invited into his world. The world remains mysterious, but as he invites me in, I am also more captivated by it.

One of the traditional tasks of a father—discipline—is also a mystery to me. Discipline is not my favorite task as a parent, but it accompanies every one of my days in some way, whether I'm enforcing bedtime or taking away my kid's privileges because of an outburst of disrespectful behavior. Parents live into their calling as they set limits for their children. In a society that often seems to live without limits (inordinate consumerism, rampant household debt, and our insatiable capacity to want more), parental discipline is even more critical. Discipline is shared in our house. I am no more the disciplinarian than Molly is, but some of my attempts at discipline have become the material of family jokes. I can lose my patience when Grace and Finn test boundaries. They sometimes pretend not to hear me when I say, "Turn the TV off." They have climbed on the countertops when told explicitly not to. They have continued to make noise and turn on the lights when it's "lights out." And on occasion I have lost my patience and yelled. Those outbursts have earned me the title Mean Man. If they hear me stomping down the hallway, they have been known to blurt out, "Look out, Mean Man's coming!" This often diffuses the tension, but sometimes it can also make me more annoyed. Yet in these little exchanges, our children put me face-to-face with my own foibles as a father; the attempts to set limits as well as my impatient streak; my own ability to laugh and the temper that is sometimes short. When I discipline, sometimes I also understand myself a little better, even if the way of discipline continues to remain mysterious.

As I discipline our children, by setting limits, by letting them know they have overstepped lines of respect, by having them experience consequences for those occasional lapses of respect that they show, and by making known that they too have responsibilities in the family, I become even more aware of the delicate nature of the relations that constitute family. I do not know why our children act in unexpected ways; I do not always fully understand my own reactions to their behavior. But we do somehow, through it all, learn more about this common business of living together, and what it means to be open to the surprise of one another each day. When a father disciplines children, he is less the maintainer of order or rule giver and more steward of the mystery of relation. A father disciplines not to mold children in his own image but to nurture them into the people they are called to become, persons who are responsive to others. Discipline too teaches us that we are not alone. As we discipline children, they also have much to teach us.

Mystery stands at the center of Christian faith. Mystery is first and foremost a mark of God, of One whose being is ineffable and beyond all words. Cosmic history begins and ends with Mystery: God is both the Ground of all that is and the culmination of all that will be. The universe finds its origin and its consummation in God's life that is the Giver and Sustainer of all life. God is Holy Mystery, the grace that surrounds life in its entirety.

Christian theology has not only stressed that the *being* of God is mystery, but that God's providence, the working out of God's purposes in history, is also mystery. God's ways are not our ways, and those ways may confound us. We often cannot readily discern the hand of God in worldly events, as if God were a puppeteer pulling strings on inert beings. There are no guarantees that human creatures will glimpse God's purposes or solve the mystery of God's activity in history. But as people of faith, we are confident that tragedy, evil, and sin will not have the final word. God will accomplish God's purposes, reveal God's love, and show those purposes and that love in concrete events both grand and small. Wherever persons are opened to the beauty and love of another person, whenever we are struck by the beauty of creation, whenever out of compassion and justice we are moved to seek the well-being of someone other than ourselves, we are also encountering the mystery of God. God's mystery does not remain enclosed upon itself but discloses itself to others in love, in history.

Another way of expressing this conviction is to say that mystery is *revealed* as God accomplishes God's purposes in history. William Clark expresses it this way: "In Christian theology, therefore, a 'mystery' is much more than 'something that cannot be understood,' but rather designates a truth that is revealed within a relationship of faith with God and grasped 'from the inside' rather than by an external analysis."[4] God reveals mystery in relation to people, and most expressly in the person of Jesus Christ, who is the embodiment of God's love for the world. For Christians, God's mystery is not an impenetrable cloud, but a *person* who reveals God's ways for the world in his acts and presence. Mystery is less an idea than it is a living relationship with the One who shows us the way to God and the nature of God. Jesus Christ does not solve the riddle of God's mystery for us but reveals mystery as a relationship that will always exhaust our words for it. In faith, Christians live into the mystery of God and do not capture or resolve it. Mystery is ongoing, dynamic, opening us to new horizons

4. Clark, "Mystery," 923.

and experiences in the journey of faith. Without that dynamism, mystery disappears and we cling to idols. Those who follow Jesus are invited not into the certainty of absolute statements that cannot be questioned (analogously to a domineering Father who brooks no questions), but into a relationship with the living God who is continually inviting us home, showing us God's love and God's will (as Jesus's narration of the prodigal son and his father indicates). In the Christian life, mystery intensifies as time goes by, since there are always new dimensions of the relationship with God yet to be lived into, yet to be shown, yet to be disclosed. God is the Mystery who keeps revealing Godself in relationship (and who in the Triune life is relationship itself).

A Christian understanding of mystery, in other words, has everything to do with relationships: God's relation with the world, our relation to one another, even fathers' relations to their children. The journey of human fathers, when we pay attention to it, shows us that as time goes by, our children become both more familiar to us and more mysterious at the same time. In an age that has well documented the pitfalls of the church's near-exclusive use of Father-language for God, one place to begin theological reflection on the human experience of fathering is to reflect on the mystery of fatherhood anew. As we engage in the work of fathering, we are also awakened by the mystery of relation. The God who is both Father and Mother invites us into the mystery of faith, a living relationship. Christian faith, in other words, gets lived out in myriad ways: at work and at play, in marriage and in friendship, as father and child. That faith does not turn us away from the ordinary relationships of human life, but invites us to encounter God in the center of them, as Holy Mystery brings new life and new things out of the ordinary in Jesus Christ. For fathers, this means that our journey with children is sacred work: familiar and mysterious, ordinary and extraordinary, at the same time. In the everyday labors of parenting, in their foibles and faults, wonder and surprise, beauty and happiness, travail and joy, we encounter God in our midst. Mystery, for fathers and children, is revealed in relation. And that makes a world of difference.

3

Sending Your Heart into the World

MARTIN B. COPENHAVER

Expecting is an odd verb to use in reference to pregnancy, particularly pregnancy with a first child, because there is so much you cannot expect. You cannot expect what the child will be like. These days you can choose to learn the sex of your child before she is born, but you cannot know other important things like her temperament, her gifts, her challenges. Before your first child is born you cannot expect how much your life will instantly and permanently change. Even if other parents try to prepare you, no one can help you anticipate fully what it is like to be a parent, any more than an unborn child can anticipate what life is like outside the womb. And you cannot expect fully how much you will be besotted with love for this new being. No one can be prepared for such signal intoxication.

For me, perhaps the biggest sucker punch of fatherhood—the one I didn't see coming and which sent me reeling—is how much having a child made me feel vulnerable to the hurts of the world. Before our two children were born, the world and the people in it seemed to have limited power to hurt me. I faced risks with a certain equanimity. After all, what's the worst that could happen? Of course, I experienced sorrows and disappointments, but even the power of those seemed limited. I figured that, for the most part, I could always bounce back or simply move on.

That changed when I became a father, and right from the start. A day or two after our first child, Alanna, was born, we brought her home from the hospital. We placed her in a big plastic bucket they gave us, an early prototype of a car seat. It was battleship gray and seemed as sturdy as a battleship also. We filled it with a nest of brightly colored blankets and pillows so that she would stay warm. (After all, this was September in New England. Who knows what severe weather might bear down on her at any moment?) And, besides, those blankets and pillows kept her head, smaller than a grapefruit, from flopping around. I'm sure that, if we had any, we also would have used some of those Styrofoam peanuts that are used for packing fragile and precious items. We buckled that car seat in just right and made sure it was secure, as carefully as if we were preparing to send her to the moon in a space capsule. I then drove the familiar roads home, but more slowly than I had ever driven them before—so slowly, in fact, that my wife, Karen, suggested I put on the flashing hazard lights to announce our pokey presence to one and all.

Gratefully, it turns out I did not become one of those "helicopter parents" who, out of an overweening protectiveness, hover so closely over their children. But it is also true that, once our children were born, no longer did I feel largely impervious to hurt. Through my children, it felt like my own naked and vulnerable heart had been sent into the world. I began to worry as I never had before because I worried about them. Through the new eyes of fatherhood, I began to see all the ways someone can be wounded. The world began to seem like a much more threatening place than it did before. And so did death.

Most parents seem to be able to remember the time they explained to their children what is sometimes called "the facts of life." At least, I've heard many such stories from parents, mostly humorous stories filled with awkward miscues from the parents and funny misunderstandings from their children. I don't recall much about such conversations with my own children—except, as I recall, their frequent use of words like *yuck*.

What I do remember with blazing clarity, however, are the conversations I had with them about, not the facts of life, but the facts of death. No one prepared me for those conversations. I never heard stories from other parents about the time their children learned that one day we die, each of us.

Alanna's first confrontation with death hit like a surprise thunderstorm. She was six years old at the time. Alanna and a little friend of hers encountered a dead frog crushed on the dirt road next to our house. At the time Alanna was, as she put it, "the master" of a pet frog. She adored that frog, so I imagine it was particularly difficult to see one of her frog's wild cousins flattened on the road. To make matters worse, her friend offered some worldly commentary: "There's nothing to get upset about. Everyone ends up like that . . . you, that frog, your mother, your father, your brother . . . " (I never did like that kid.)

Alanna responded by running home in tears. I still remember—without wanting to remember—the grief-stricken look on her face as she burst through the door. I remember scrambling to find something to say, desperately trying to control a conflagration of grief when it felt like all I had was a teaspoon with which to douse it. I held her as she cried for what seemed like hours. One's first encounter with death is never a trifling thing.

Never before had death seemed so much like an enemy as it did that day.

I do not remember what occasioned my conversation about death with our son, Todd, when he was about the same age Alanna had been. But I do remember that he, too, wept with great swelling sobs that lasted for a very long time and seemed to come from a depth that had not been tapped before or since. I also remember searching for something to say, something that would be both reassuring and true. I remember saying that death is not something to fear, even though I cannot tell you exactly what it will be like. I said that God takes care of us in death, even as God takes care of us in life. I tried to assure him that, in some mysterious way we cannot fully imagine, we will live even after we die. My words continued to flow, and so did Todd's tears. Such a huge reality. Such a little boy.

I wanted to protect my children not only from death but also from the thought of death. I also did not want them to have to experience the hurt of hot words or frozen silences, or betrayals, both large and small, or loneliness, grief, failure, rejection, disappointment, not to mention injury and disease.

To be sure, all of those things are part of life—inevitably so. And I am even aware of ways those experiences can enrich a life. "I know that," the father says with his head but not his heart. You see, when it comes to my children, I would prefer to have all of those experiences just pass by on the other side of the street.

For a number of years Todd spent a month at a summer camp for boys in the Adirondack Mountains. I had attended the same camp when I was a boy. It was that kind of place—the camp, and the love of it, passed down from one generation to another like a treasured inheritance.

That first summer we wanted to make sure that we heard from Todd, who hated to write, so the first season he went to camp we bribed him. For every note he sent home, we would buy him a pack of basketball cards (he was always interested in expanding his extensive collection). If he wrote every day, he would receive thirty packs of basketball cards. It was a potential bonanza.

Weeks passed. No cards or letters home. Our concern mounted. Then, a day or two before we were to pick him up, a lumpy envelope arrived. In it was a collection of small scraps of paper—some of them as small as the fortune you find in a cookie—one for each day. Most of his notes were as brief as haiku poems: "Went fishing. Caught nothing. What a perfect day." He had been so joyfully engaged in the activities of the camp that he didn't want to take the time to write, but he didn't want to give up on the prospect of all of those basketball cards, either, so he resorted to writing micronotes.

From that first summer, the camp had become Todd's special place. It was a joy to see him head to camp, knowing that he felt embraced by the place and the people he knew there. As he got older his notes home, almost always ebullient, even got longer.

But then, one summer—Todd was fourteen—the notes home became infrequent and their tone was flat. One evening we got a phone call from Todd, which was unusual because campers needed special permission to call.

"How are things going?" one of us asked.

He replied with a bit of a crack in his voice: "All right, I guess. I gave the vespers meditation before lights out. I told my cabin that I don't think it's right for someone to be called gay as a put down, that there is nothing wrong with being gay."

Our congregation had just completed a process to declare ourselves as affirming of all people, regardless of sexual orientation. This was at a time when there still was not consensus on that matter within our tradition—or in our congregation—so it had not been an easy process. I had strong convictions on the subject, so I did not doubt that we should move forward. But I only had to work with a group of adults. To challenge a cabin full of fourteen-year-old boys on this subject was another matter.

Karen asked, "How'd they take it?"

A long pause. "They didn't get it. No one really understood what I was trying to say. They still don't get it."

"Do they tease you about it?" I asked, afraid that I already knew the answer.

"What do you think?" is all he said in reply.

I was proud of him, and told him so. What I did not tell him is that I did not want him to have to make sacrifices for his convictions. And this was not a large sacrifice, in the scheme of things, just some teasing from some boys in your cabin. It was just one of those small childhood bruises. Todd bounced back from the experience quickly. So why does the pain I heard in his voice continue to whisper in my ear?

Protecting our children from hurt is not always a selfless act. Sometimes when we seem to be protecting our children, we are actually trying to protect ourselves from the hurt we experience through them.

When Alanna was in college, she spent a summer in Johannesburg, South Africa. She went as an intern for Gun Free South Africa, an organization that seeks to address the huge problem of gun violence in that young country. From the beginning she was so excited about going, even though she did not know a soul there.

Johannesburg is enormous, gritty, and one of the most dangerous cities in the world. Alanna had barely landed—she had not even arrived at the home where she was to stay—when someone tried to snatch her purse. Each day she would ride a bus to work. People in Johannesburg don't talk on their cell phones while on the bus or on the streets because that would invite theft, often at gunpoint.

Knowing the dangers of that city, one church member asked me why on earth we let her go. I said that in some way Alanna felt called to go. I pulled out a quote I read somewhere: "A ship is safe in harbor, but that's not what ships are for." I tried humor: "We taught her to be committed to social justice. It is hard when our children don't listen to us. But sometimes it is a lot harder when they do." I don't think any of my responses satisfied her, because they didn't entirely satisfy me.

I visited Alanna while she was in Johannesburg, in large part to be a witness to what was so obviously a significant experience in her life. I arrived after two red-eye flights in a row, having slept very little, but I was energized at the prospect of seeing Alanna and to know, in ways I could not by e-mail, that she was fine.

Alanna had planned out practically every hour of the week we would spend together. My first night we joined a church group in feeding homeless folks on the streets of the city, something Alanna had done several times before I had arrived. In the basement of the downtown church, we met about twenty others who going to serve that night. We were the only Americans. We piled into one of two vans, each with a huge vat of soup and loaves of bread, and drove off in separate directions.

Several blocks from the church our van was in a neighborhood I would normally not feel safe even driving through. It was dark, except for occasional small bonfires on the streets. The buildings looked as if they had been bombed. Some windows remained, but they were all broken. Many of the brick walls had collapsed, or looked as if they were about to. Very few people were on the streets. Those who ventured out were almost all young men. The streets smelled of urine.

Then we pulled up to a building that didn't look any different from the others. I wondered why we were stopping there because I didn't see anyone on the streets. Alanna said, "This is it. We go in this building." And then she hopped out of the van, as if she had just been dropped off at a party. She was the first one in our group to get a Styrofoam cup of soup in each hand, with a couple of slices of bread placed on top. Then I was next.

When I had my two cups of soup, Alanna said, "Okay, we go in here," nodding to the bombed-out building.

Everything seemed to be happening so fast, but when she said that, everything also seemed to hold still for a long moment as my mind struggled to take it all in and to regain some kind of equilibrium. Under normal circumstances, there is no way that I would let my daughter go near this place. I would never choose to let my naked and vulnerable heart be sent to such a place. But she was walking through an opening in the wall of the building. Probably once it was a proper doorway, but now it was so rough and disheveled that it looked something like the entrance of a cave. As she walked through the opening, the darkness immediately swallowed her. I followed.

Inside, it took a while for our eyes to adjust to the darkness. The only source of light was a small fire around which about ten men were gathered. Most of the interior walls had been torn down, so we could see dimly other clusters of men in other parts of the enormous room.

Alanna walked up to the group around the fire, handed soup to two of the men and began chatting with them, as naturally as if this were a coffee hour after worship at our church in suburban Boston.

I am sure that my faith has informed my vocation as a father. But I am also keenly aware of how my experience as a father has informed my faith. For one, I think I understand—still dimly, but almost at a visceral level—some of the implications of the affirmation that God sent his own child into the world. Before Jesus, the ways in which God could experience fear or hurt or sorrow were limited. But all that changed with Jesus.

That is, in Jesus, God sent his own naked and vulnerable heart into the world.

4

Learning from My Kids: A Father's Story

GREG GARRETT

It's March in Oklahoma City, Oklahoma, a gray day, but warmer than it has been for a week, and the snow that lies piled up on the lawns and medians has begun to melt. Jake, my only son, is three years old, and after all this time snowbound, we're finally together and headed to the park on our Wednesday afternoon. His mom and I are divorced, but I get to see him every Wednesday for four hours, and every other weekend. I live for these Wednesdays, plunked down as they are in the middle of a week when I am a full-time PhD student and a full-time lecturer teaching five classes at a local university. I don't know how this is even possible, and if I stopped to think about it, I'm sure the whole house of cards would collapse. What matters is that every Wednesday I have time with Jake where I can forget everything else I'm supposed to be doing and just be present with him.

At least, that's how it works in theory. In reality, I am often in my head, thinking about something else, worried or obsessed about all that needs to be done after I take him home.

On this particular afternoon, we are going to the School Park. Jake identifies each park we visit on Wednesdays based on some distinguishing characteristic. There's the Big Slide Park, a neighborhood park named—you guessed it—for a tall slide that he squeals when he goes down; there's the Sticker Park, a municipal park whose straggly lawn features way too many sand burrs. This is the School Park because it's the playground behind an elementary school, and Jake likes it because it has a massive playscape with slides and bridges and multiple levels, all sorts of places to climb and jump and swing and sway.

Jake is only three, but he is solid, a lump of muscle and bone. When he was born, he weighed eleven pounds, seven ounces, and the nurses throughout the hospital came up to the room to see him with their own eyes. They called him "Rocky," because the little mitts put on him to keep him from scratching himself looked like boxing gloves—like he could take on a two-year-old and win by TKO. He comes by this build naturally, partly his mom's genes, partly my Grandpa Chuck, who is over six feet and well built. His mom was All State in tennis and basketball, started on a state-championship basketball team; Jake is going to have her athletic genes and the frame of a linebacker.

We are driving through the slush to the School Park in my new red Beretta. I've only had it for a week. I've just replaced the battered Chevy Citation that almost never started unless I parked it on an incline so I could pop the clutch. This is the one positive thing I can say about my impossible job as lecturer: I can afford this car. To say I am proud and protective of my Beretta does not do justice to what I'm feeling; you would have to have driven a succession of crappy and unreliable cars, have to have been scoffed at by fellow motorists and scorned by beautiful girls. My old Citation burned a quart of oil a week, and left the car behind me in a roiling cloud of black smoke whenever I pulled away from a stoplight.

It was no way to win friends and influence people.

So I am over the moon proud that I can afford this car now, and when I picked up Jake earlier, we actually had a come-to-Jesus reminder session about car etiquette and three-year-olds.

"This is our new car," I told him then.

"The red race car," he affirmed, smiling like a jack-o'-lantern.

"Yes," I smiled back. "The red race car. Do you like it?"

He nodded, big affirmative motions of his head.

"Then you know why we don't drink in the new car. We don't eat in the new car. We don't get snow or mud in the new car. We're trying very hard to keep this car clean and sparkly. Do you understand?"

Jake nodded again firmly. He was on board.

Still, I am crazy about this car, so when we arrive at the School Park and I see the melting snow and resulting muck, I give him firm instructions: "We're walking on the sidewalk all the way to the playground. Not on the grass. We don't want to get mud in the new car, do we?"

Jake shakes his head, and again it is firmly. No, he does not.

I slip his mittens and hat on, pull him out of his booster seat on the passenger side. Then I zip up his jacket, and we walk, purposefully, along the sidewalk out to the distant playscape, his mittened hand in mine.

Once there, Jake climbs up the playscape, and I step back to get a better vantage point. I like to watch him play. Jake runs across bridges and slides down slides. He climbs ladders. I throw soggy snowballs at him, and he runs, squealing with joy. One splatters against the back of his jacket, and I make a mental note to dry him off before we get back in the car.

And while I'm thinking that, he climbs to the edge of one of the units and decides he wants to jump across to the other, and before I can even call out a word of warning, he jumps, misses his hold, and falls, hitting his head on the wooden lower level with a loud *thunk* that sends a chill through me.

Instantly, Jake lets out a wail of pain, and I run across to him, scoop him up, see the blood pouring out of the cut on his scalp. I am filled with fear—it's a lot of blood, and although I take off my sweatshirt and try to staunch the flow, it keeps coming. Underneath my hand, my shirt is turning red.

And so I scoop Jake up in my arms and run directly for the car, my feet sinking ankle deep in the mud of the field as we go.

"Daddy," Jake wails as we cut across the field. I can feel the mud clinging to the bottom of my feet, more with each step.

"What, baby?" I look down at him. There is blood all over his face, and I think, *He must be scared. He must be so scared.*

If he is anywhere near as scared as I am, he must, in fact, be petrified.

"Daddy!" he screams again. He is trying to get my attention.

"What?" I repeat. I am more than halfway across the field now, and starting to juggle him in my arms so I can pull the keys out of my pocket and get us instantly underway.

"You said we were supposed to stay on the sidewalk," he wails. "You're going to get the new car all dirty!"

I almost stop dead in the field. Under less extreme circumstances, I feel certain I would have.

I feel something warm and runny break loose inside me: love, and shame, and a tangle of other emotions oozing into my rib cage.

I am still moving through the muddy field, but I look down at him, and I am crying now, crying like him, if for a very different reason.

"I know," I say, stepping onto the pavement of the parking lot, the mud heavy on the bottom of my shoes. "I know I told you we needed to take care of the new car. But you are more important. People are always more important."

I belt him into the booster seat.

I climb into the driver's seat, my feet inches thick with mud, turn the key in the ignition, feel my foot slide onto the gas pedal.

And I go squealing out of the parking lot to get help for my child.

"How do you describe yourself?" a friend of mine asked me the other day. She was referring to the multiple vocations of writer, teacher, speaker, and preacher by which she knows me. It is those things that are always first in the public eye, the way I'm introduced when I speak or do media, the way I describe myself on my Facebook profile, which is largely for readers and fans. But honesty compels me, when I introduce myself to people to whom I want to be known as a human being and not as an Author or Professional Christian, to add "partner" and "father" to that list, to bump those up to the top, in fact; for although I exist in the world's eyes largely in terms of that first set of vocational nouns, I exist in the eyes of those I love—and of myself—primarily in the second relational set.

Of all the titles I hold, none defines me more.

Like some men, I didn't come to fatherhood with enthusiasm; I had things I wanted to do, places I wanted to go, and I knew without doubt that to be a father—to really be a father—would tie me down in ways I couldn't yet name. I had accumulated a hefty dose of selfishness from being the oldest child in a large family, forever responsible for others, and wondering when I was going to have time for myself. Vistas opened in front of me: a creative-writing teacher wanted me to do graduate work at Cornell, and I saw myself in tweed jackets with patches at the elbows; a touring rock band asked me to go on the road with them as their lead singer, and I had a now-disturbing image of me in leopard-print pants twirling a microphone stand.

But my own choices—and maybe, if I'm honest, my own fear of failure—kept my dreams closer to home, in small-town Oklahoma. I married my high school sweetheart, and shortly after, I learned that although we had agreed to put off children for a while, she was pregnant.

"How did that happen?" I asked (which, guys, if you should ever wonder, is precisely the wrong thing to say in response to the happy news).

"I went off the pill," she told me, defiant and offended. "Months ago."

So, there it was. I hadn't chosen to be a father, but I was going to be one. Honesty again compels me to admit: I was not excited. I was resentful. I was apprehensive about how I was going to finish college with a family to support, and I was more than a little scared that I would screw this up. I mean, look how I'd responded to my wife when she told me she was going to bear my child! Does that sound like the voice of a good family man?

Late at night, about six weeks into the pregnancy, I heard my wife weeping in the bathroom. She had complained of sharp cramps before bed, and I could see the fear in her eyes when she turned out the light. When I found her in the bathroom, the stool bloody, those fears were realized.

As occurs in roughly 20 percent of all pregnancies, she had miscarried, and she looked up at me with tears in her eyes, defiant and offended.

"Well," she said. "I hope you're happy now."

Sure.

Right.

Happiness has often been an elusive concept for me, although satisfaction is much more familiar, and the pleasure of doing something you said you would do has long been one of my driving motivations. I come from a long line of hard-working men. On my mother's side, there was her father, Chuck, who was a farmer and rancher in northwest Oklahoma, who got up—literally—at dawn and worked until dusk, who had already been out to feed the cattle before I got up to have breakfast, who drove tractors and combines, who made things grow. On my father's side was my adoptive grandfather, Orval, a handyman who was constantly in motion, who could fix a door or a carburetor or an elevator, who could do magic with his hands.

My father is largely a void in the memory of my childhood. That doesn't mean I didn't love him—I did, and I do—but it does mean I think of him as largely AWAY: traveling on business when I was very young and we lived in the South, working late when I was older and he was state claims manager for Allstate Insurance in Oklahoma. At seventy-five he still works as many hours as I do in all my jobs together, is still settling claims. He climbs roofs; he checks burnt-out houses for signs of arson; he assigns lawyers to cases that don't seem quite right; and he chats up clients, claimants, and everyone else in the vicinity. I don't think he will ever slow down.

As I said, I love my father, but absence is not the greatest teacher of how to *be* one, and after he and my mother divorced, although we had more intentional time together, we were buddies, not father and son. So

I took affection from my sweet and funny Grandpa Orval, felt the steady support of my Grandpa Chuck, and tried to cobble together images of a father wherever I could. Sometimes that impulse led to strong and lasting relationships. I still communicate with my high school choir director, Mr. Beach, who offered me a scholarship to sing in his college choir after he became Dr. Beach, and who loved me not just for my talent but because he saw something in me worth nurturing.

Sometimes that search for a father figure led to disaster. Another man who mentored me, offered me living space in his house after Jake's mom and I finally divorced, and made himself indispensable to me, turned out to be a sexual predator interested in other things besides my potential.

It's a dangerous thing to want and need a father, and so important to have a clear concept of who a father is and what he does, especially if you're going to have to be one. Not long after our miscarriage, Jake's mom got pregnant again and carried Jake to term. And there I was, a prospective father whose best images of what good fathers looked like were drawn from grandparents or from pop culture—the stolid father of *Father Knows Best*, the hip laid-back Mike Brady.

After Jake was born, you can see the mingled joy and apprehension in my eyes in the first picture where I am holding him, the fear that I have no idea what I'm doing.

Little did I know that eventually my children would teach me what I needed to know about being their father—and many of the things I needed to know about what matters in life.

It's July in Austin, Texas, the kind of hot and sunny day that Texans know all too well: hundred-degree heat and scorching pavement, or—if you're at the seminary pool, as my son Chandler and I are—bath-warm water and potential sunburn.

Chandler is eight years old, slender and small-boned like his mother, a dancer instead of a linebacker like his brother, Jake. They differ in other ways, as well. Chandler has been a smart and demanding child almost from the day he emerged into my hands. Whereas Jake is the textbook definition of laid back, as a baby, a child, and now, as a man, Chandler is energetic and strong willed. Even when he was a baby, he would wear you down. You could not outwait his cries; he would make you give in. And there was nothing easy about him—not feeding him, not getting him to sleep. I would try to put him down, since his mom would wake to feed him, and it required a heroic effort: an hour of humming and dancing with him in my arms, listening to the David Crowder Band, which he seemed to like, or to smooth jazz.

And then in the night he would wake—once, twice, more often. We tried the family bed, but I was a bad sleeper at the best of times, and I was, again, the one who broke. I abandoned the family bed for the guest room, where I still woke every time he did—although at least not every time he moved.

Those were bad times in every part of my life, and my memories of Chandler's childhood are mostly missing, along with most of my other memories. But now at the pool, it is the summer of 2005, and I am well, and attending seminary at the Episcopal Theological Seminary of the Southwest full time while I continue to teach full time at Baylor, and Chandler is in the pool with his friends: with Natalie and Georgia, whose parents are from Memphis; with Mikalee and Samantha, whose parents are from Kansas City; with Lev, whose father is my theology professor.

"Get in!" Chandler keeps calling to me. The kids are splashing in delight, and there is a pool full of toys, and I can't see how I could possibly add anything to their experience. Although sweat is running down my face, I have a cup full of cold beer, and I am talking with my friend, Don, who is my seminary classmate and the father of Natalie and Georgia, and who at this moment is telling me how sorry he feels for any man who marries Natalie; for Natalie, like Chandler, is strong willed, opinionated, and very good looking.

We have too few chances to just sit, Don and I, and although I would like to be fully present, I am also thinking about all the things I need to do. I am taking Greek this summer, and it is a monster. I am wondering about my classes for the fall semester at Baylor, and about the seminary fieldwork I will begin in September: I will be serving for two years in a rural parish, working every Sunday as teacher or preacher or server at the altar.

I am worrying about next summer's Clinical Pastoral Education (CPE) where I will work full time as a hospital chaplain for four hundred hours. My friends who have done CPE have shared horror stories, and although I am a good student, I have always wondered if I will wash out of seminary because of CPE. This summer's Greek, hard as it is, is an academic subject; chaplaincy is about pastoral care—in emergencies and over the long haul and being wholly present with someone who is suffering . . .

"Get in, Dad!" Chandler calls, interrupting my thoughts, and the other kids join him in calling me into the pool: "Come on, Greg! Get in! Please!"

Now Chandler climbs up out of the pool, his suit baggy and hanging low on his hips, huge on his slender body, and he comes dripping across to where I sit.

"We want you to play with us," he says, takes my free arm, pulls.

"I'm having a good time talking to the Donald," I tell him, disengaging my arm; and I am, when we talk. Although Don and I are different in almost every way, I love him dearly, and we don't get much time to talk outside class.

But I take a sip of my beer, and it is getting warm. I have a few more swallows left, then it will be gone, and I will have to seek another.

Plus the sweat is soaking my hair, running down my back and chest, and I am hot.

The water starts to seem like a good idea.

"I'll get in the pool in just a second," I tell him, reaching my decision. "As soon as I finish my beer."

"And you'll play with us," he reminds me.

"Maybe," I say. I don't know if he has worked this out in his decade on the planet, but when I reply to any question with maybe instead of a simple yes or no, what I probably mean is, probably not.

I don't want to.

I hear, acknowledge, and do not choose to do that.

I take one more swallow of beer. Hot now. *Gaah.* I pour the rest on the grass.

I get up, take three steps, and slide into the deep end of the pool, sinking down past the warm upper layer and into the cool water in the depths.

When I am ready to come up, I push off toward the shallow end.

"Play with us," Chandler says, when I bob up next to him. There are encouraging similar shouts.

"I don't think so," I tell him. I don't think of myself as a playful person. I have been working since I was fifteen years old, have supported a family since I was twenty-two, am probably, if I am honest, entirely too earnest and serious for my own good. While I love the outdoors, bike, and play music, thanks to my Southern Baptist upbringing I typically feel guilty when I am having a good time.

The kids are mobbing me now, grabbing my arms, tugging. If they weren't known and loved quantities, I would be afraid they were trying to drown me. "Play with us," they say. "Please!"

"Please," Chandler seconds, a brown, adorable seal, and I cannot refuse him. As usual, he outlasts me.

"What do you want to play?" I ask. And for an hour, I do whatever they suggest. We play Marco Polo, that grand game of swimming-pool tag. We play shark, Chandler swimming underwater like an otter, me the dangerous shark trying to grab him. We play light sabers, bashing each other senseless with brightly-colored foam floaties.

Finally, I throw those who want to be thrown, arcing them up out of my hands and into the deep end. Some dive. Some want to be lobbed like human logs. Some love the feeling of not knowing how they're going to fly and how they're going to land. While Chandler does not want to be thrown, he watches with joy, laughing his head off.

We all are. Every time I throw Natalie or Mikalee and they squeal as they fly through the air, every time I toss Lev and he lands loudly and gracelessly with an enormous wet splash, I throw back my head and laugh like crazy.

I have not thought about work for an hour. I have not thought about what I should be doing, or what I will be doing.

I have simply played, hard, until my arms ache and I gasp for air.

When I try to climb out of the pool, Chandler takes my arm, holds on.

"Play with us," he pleads.

"Later," I tell him. "I'm beat. You guys have worn me out." And they have.

They look back at me proudly. Playing is hard work.

And good work.

This is the first time—but most certainly not the last—that I will play hard at the pool with Chandler and these kids.

Life is too short to be so serious.

Chandler, when he came along, was not expected either, although he was, at least, not unforeseen. I had been married to his mother for a year and a half, and after a testy and stress-filled last day of cross-country travel moving from Texas to Oregon, where I would be on sabbatical, we conceived Chandler after the moving truck was unloaded—makeup sex. It was during her fertile window, and we didn't take other precautions, and these things happen, right?

When she came into our room one morning with a pregnancy test in one hand and announced that we were going to have a baby, I acquitted myself much more creditably. I reacted with enthusiasm and the appropriate tone of joy. I did early morning tamale runs. I gave back rubs. I supported her desire to have a natural childbirth, coached her during labor (until, that is, she told me that the sound of my voice made her want to kill me), caught Chandler when he was born.

I had good intentions, and felt like I had some command of this whole fatherhood thing now. When Chandler was born, Jake was twelve, and while for eight years I had only seen him once a month and for a month in the summer, I had taken care of him; fed, diapered, and bathed him; and taught him how to ride a bike; and I felt like I could bring the same skills to Chandler.

Things didn't work out the way I'd hoped. I had these fathering skills down, yes; but after Chandler was born, my life skills went missing. My chronic depression was aggravated by my now-chronic insomnia, and I fell apart. For some years in Chandler's early life, in fact, it was all I could do to hold myself together, and on more than one occasion I considered killing myself.

The boys were one of my few reasons to stay alive, although sometimes I thought even they would be better off without me. I could hardly be a good father when I wasn't a functioning human being. Still, I felt grateful for my time with the kids. I felt loved by them when I didn't even love myself. I felt the closest thing to joy that I knew in those dark days when they laughed or hugged me.

Then in 2003, I got better. Although I've written and talked about my recovery at length, to this day, a decade later, I still don't know exactly what happened. I went off my antidepressants, I haven't had a suicidal thought since, and I've lived my life with joy and with much less guilt and regret.

Certainly what happened was spiritual. Some would call it miraculous, although I make no such claim.

But the truth is, for the past decade, I have been able to be fully present for my kids: for Jake, now an adult trying to make his way in the world; for Chandler, now a teenager, trying to figure out what he's going to do with himself; and for my two beautiful girls, Lily and Sophie, the daughters of the woman I love.

I have a backlog of paternal experience now, a library of child-rearing techniques, a number of patented parenting moves.

I am as healthy emotionally and spiritually as I have ever been, and as happy in my professional and personal lives as I can remember.

Yet I am still learning spiritual lessons, now in my unfamiliar role as father to daughters, as protector, white knight, Prince Charming to two princesses.

It is Summer 2011, and we are at Phil's Icehouse, a family-friendly burger joint in north Austin: me, Jeanie, and her daughters Lily and Sophie. It is early in our life together, and the girls are still trying to figure out where I fit in the picture, what they think of me. They know that I'm not their dad—and I am not trying to replace him—but they are also figuring out that I'm more than a casual friend who dropped by for dinner.

We play hide-and-seek on the playground while we're waiting for our burgers. At four, Lily is a veteran at this game. She can hide expertly, and when it is time to look for me and two-year-old Sophie, she hunts methodically and roots us out behind the trash can or in the hedges.

Sophie squeals when Lily finds us and toddles off with the gait of a happy monkey. Sophie, for all the care she needs, is easy. She is accepting, warm. You get what you see.

Lily is like her mom, though. She is whip-smart, reserves judgment, isn't quite sure.

And right now, she still isn't quite sure about me.

I could take offense. Since I fell head over heels for their mom, I have known that I wanted to raise these girls. I have loved them with the passion that it is easy to develop for those we don't even know yet. I am still a full-time professor at Baylor, and a full-time writer, teacher, speaker, and preacher, but, now for the first time I can remember, I really want to be a full-time father and husband.

I am all in, and I want Lily to be too.

But she holds herself in reserve, looks at me with a critical eye, is still trying to figure out if I am to be trusted.

Jeanie, Lily, and Sophie share one of the monster burgers and an order of rings and curly fries. After we eat, I'll get us ice cream. I'm hoping it will be a bonding experience; who doesn't like ice cream? And after, we'll play on the playground until it gets dark. The girls will run across the playscape, maybe we'll climb on the big blue concrete cows you can see as you drive past Phil's on Burnet Road.

And so I wander onto the playground with them after we finish ice cream, while Jeanie squares things away at our table. Sophie is trying to climb onto the playscape, but Lily has stopped dead, is staring at a kid sitting on top of the big blue cow, is weighing possibilities. Someone has pulled a chair over to the side of the cow, and when this kid jumps down, Lily climbs into the chair and tries to pull herself up onto the cow's back.

She slides, can't get a purchase. She's still a little too short to make this work, but I stand back to see if she can do it herself. She is intent and intense, studying the problem, determined to solve it on her own.

At last, she slides back down, shakes her head, and turns to me and asks, "Can you help me, Greg?"

I smile and nod. I pick her up and place her on top of the cow's back. She smiles too, radiant, the contrast so marked between this expression and the intense thinking grimace of a few moments earlier.

"Do you want to sit on the cow's head?" I ask, after she's had time to look around and survey her kingdom.

She reflects a moment, then nods, big affirmative motions of her head. I pick her up again and place her atop the cow's head, about five feet off the ground. I hold her with one hand, just at her left side, to keep her stable, and she smiles big and calls out to Jeanie to take a look. "Mommy! Mommy!"

When at last it's time to come off, she looks down, considers the possibilities, makes that thoughtful face again, and I suggest, "I'll fly you down."

She considers for a moment. It's a reflection I know all too well. The world can be a dangerous place, and not everyone I have ever trusted has proven worthy of it.

We can hold ourselves in reserve, afraid to love, afraid to commit.

We can think our only safety is in ourselves, which is also an illusion.

Or we can take a leap of faith.

"Fly me," Lily says, and as I move my hands up under her arms she lays her hands on them.

"Don't let go," she says, as though that needs be emphasized.

"I won't," I tell her.

She nods.

I pick her up and launch her into space, and she makes a keening noise of joy as I fly her through the air and deposit her some distance from the cow, set her down near Sophie and the playscape filled with kids.

She pauses for a moment squatting there as she landed, my hands still holding her, and then her face lights up.

"Again!" she says.

"Okay," I say. I feel something liquid flooding into my chest—something like love and joy and relief and hope all at once. For the first time in something besides my dreams, I see myself reading Lily to sleep, packing her school lunch, arguing with her about her math problems and knowing she is probably right.

I imagine the harrowing interview I am going to concoct for her poor suitors ten years from now.

It has taken me a long time to learn to be the father I am now, and I know I am still learning as father and as human being, still learning how to prioritize, to love, to trust.

But I have learned much, at last, to my own continuing surprise.

And often, I have learned by watching and by listening to the children I love.

"Don't let go," Lily repeats now, as I carry her back over to the blue cow, as I set her atop its head, as I prepare to launch her into flight again.

"I won't," I tell her, as I will tell her as many times as it needs to be said. "You know I won't."

"Okay," she says, shivering with anticipatory delight. She looks me over, smiles big, nods. She is ready.

"Fly me, Greg."

And I do.

I do.

5

Remembering a Father, Becoming a Father

ALBERT Y. HSU

My dad, Terry Tsai-Yuan Hsu, was born in Taiwan in 1939 during the era of Japanese occupation prior to World War II. He was poor but excelled in school, eventually scoring as one of the top ten students in the country on a national college entrance exam. He went to Taiwan's best university and then came to the United States in the 1960s to do his master's and doctorate in electrical engineering.

I was born in 1972 in New York City, while my dad was earning his PhD at City College of New York. I don't remember very much of those early years, but I do recall that once when I was two or three years old, I stuck a fork into a rotary fan, shattering the blades. My dad spanked me. There must be something about childhood punishment that imprints itself upon one's memory, because my mental picture of that apartment comes from that scene.

My dad finished his dissertation in 1976, and he got a job in Minnesota. So we moved to the Twin Cities metropolitan area and eventually settled in Bloomington, a suburb of Minneapolis. I grew up watching reruns of *Leave It to Beaver* and *The Brady Bunch.* And one of my early childhood realizations was that my family was not like these happy white families on TV. We were one of the only Asian American families in our community; at the time, Minnesota was something like 98 percent white. I was one of the only nonwhite kids in my school.

Besides experiencing various degrees of childhood teasing, stereotyping, and racial marginalization, I gradually became aware of a significant cultural difference between my family and the others around us. These white American families actually talked to each other. Parents and children interacted with one another. Those clean-cut Cleavers, those happy Brady kids, my classmates and neighbors down the block, they had family situations where fathers would talk to their kids in actual conversation, imparting moral wisdom or guidance, providing life lessons.

This was not the case in my family. My relationship with my father was complicated. He wasn't an absent father, like so many today—he was always present. He had a 9-to-5 job and was always home for dinner. But he was seemingly unapproachable. He didn't initiate conversation with me.

My dad was mostly silent, stoic, not much for conversation. Compared to American dads, my father seemed reserved and distant. He didn't talk much with me, and he certainly didn't express affection. He never said things like "I love you." The Bradys told each other these things all the time, seemingly every episode. Why not my dad? Did he not like me?

In retrospect now, I recognize that probably a function of Confucian Chinese/Taiwanese cultural values was that parents, and especially fathers, simply did not express their emotions in such ways. Fathers and sons are not peers and do not communicate as if they are equals. Filial piety and respect require fathers to hold themselves at a distance from their children. In addition, my dad was also an introvert, and he kept most of his thoughts and feelings internalized.

I recognize now that many white American kids also had difficult relationships with absentee fathers. But whereas many of my friends' dads at least played catch with them and taught them how to play baseball or football, my dad rarely did anything like that with me. I only recall him playing catch with me once or twice. My dad was into tennis more than baseball, and he did try to play tennis with me on occasion. But he stopped bothering because I was not able to play competitively against him, so it wasn't worth the effort or time.

I remember once, perhaps during my junior high years, I saw a TV show where a kid said to his dad, "Dad, I don't like you." The father looked crestfallen, until the kid said, "I don't like you—I *love* you!" The father smiled broadly, and there were big hugs all around.

For some reason I decided to try this with my own dad. So as he was sitting at his desk, reading his Chinese newspaper, I went up to him and said, "Dad, I don't like you." He glared at me and said, "Well, you can just leave."

Taken aback, I continued with, "I *love* you . . ." but my heart wasn't in it anymore. I felt foolish for even trying; I should have known that my family wasn't like the ones on TV.

≈

When I graduated from grad school with my master's degree, my dad gave me a watch as a graduation gift. I've worn it pretty much every day since. At the time I thought it would be a reminder of my degree, a marker of my academic milestone. But now it's a reminder of him, and also of the uncertainty of life and how none of us knows how much time we will have with our loved ones.

Shortly after my wife and I got married, my father had a stroke. He survived the stroke, but it left him partly debilitated on the left side of his body. He started rehab and physical therapy and was making progress, but one of the side effects was that he spun into a severe depression. He lost all sense of hope. Three months after the stroke, he took his own life, strangling himself with a coat hanger. He was fifty-eight years old.

A few months after my father's death, I had a phone conversation with my mother and we talked about my dad. We were both still in the immediacy of the grieving process. In tears, she confessed something to me that I had never known about my parents. She said, "He made me have an abortion."

Apparently it had happened during my dad's PhD work in New York. I was still a toddler when my mother had gotten pregnant again. My dad said that he didn't want another crying baby distracting him from his studies. So they had an abortion.

I vaguely knew that my mother had had a miscarriage or two sometime when I was younger, but I hadn't known anything about the details. Now I wondered about this unborn sibling of mine. I could have had another brother or sister. What would he or she have been like? How would our family have been different if I had grown up with this other person? How could they have terminated him or her? How could my father have forced my mother to take their child's life?

My parents eventually did have another son; my brother Ed was born ten years after I came along. I remember being an only child during my early elementary years and asking my parents why I didn't have a brother or sister. I think I may have just wanted a playmate, or perhaps I wanted my parents to focus on someone else besides me. After Ed arrived, I soon became a teenager and saw my kid brother as more of a pest than the pal I had long awaited. Now I wonder if they had him partly out of guilt, to atone for the child they had aborted years earlier.

≈

The biggest difference between my father and me is that he had no religious faith or commitments of any kind, apart from a scientific materialism and general agnosticism about anything supernatural. I on the other hand have been a professing evangelical Christian since my midteens. My mother, a Christian, had taken me to church and Sunday school and Vacation Bible School and church camps along the way. It was interesting to have the contrast between my parents. On Sunday mornings, I had the choice to go to church with my mom or stay home with my dad. I could see the differences in their lifestyles and worldviews, and I could decide for myself which path I wanted to take.

I chose to my mother's path, and I chose to follow Jesus. This was the biggest bone of contention between me and my father during my teenage years and into my twenties. We had many arguments about the existence of God and the validity of the Christian faith. He was disappointed that I chose to go to a Christian college and felt that I was wasting my time and education. I considered seminary, but he said that I should go to graduate school instead, since a communications degree would be more practically useful than knowing ancient biblical languages.

Eventually I think he came to some degree of acceptance of my life trajectory. He may have still thought that I had been brainwashed by a religious cult, but he said that I could do what I wanted to do, that I didn't have to try to please him. I never truly got a sense of blessing from him, but I knew that he was at least glad that I had turned out okay.

He lived long enough to come to my wedding and to see the publication of my first book; he died just a few months afterward. He never met my own sons, Josiah and Elijah, who only know him from pictures and stories.

I lament the fact that my boys do not know their grandfather. I grieve his absence as a loss. I wonder how he would have interacted with them, if he would have played games with them or read books to them. Once when we visited his gravesite, I told my father that he would have been proud of Josiah, that Josiah loves to build things with Legos, and that Josiah must have inherited some of his engineering skills from him.

I also wonder what he would have thought of my younger son, Elijah. I wonder what he would have thought of our decision to have him.

$$\approx$$

Halfway into our second pregnancy, my wife, Ellen, and I were alerted that our unborn child had certain "abnormalities." The doctor doing the ultrasound pointed out physical markers that seemed to indicate possible club feet, cleft palate, problems with the spine and vital organs. He suspected Trisomy 13 or 18, genetic conditions that were "incompatible with life." He told us, "Based on this information, you can decide to terminate the pregnancy."

We were stunned. Our first pregnancy had had no problems, and we had delivered a healthy son, Josiah. What had gone wrong this time? Would we be planning for a funeral rather than a birth?

We had an amniocentesis done, at which point they confirmed that our son would have Down syndrome, Trisomy 21. On the one hand, we were relieved that this was not as serious as other more life-threatening conditions. On the other hand, we still faced uncertainty, likely many medical challenges, and perhaps a lifetime of special-needs care. We talked with a colleague who has a granddaughter with Down syndrome, and he mentioned that his first reaction was that his daughter and son-in-law may never have an empty nest. We also heard a statistic that about 90 percent of couples who have a prenatal diagnosis of Down syndrome choose to terminate.

I don't recall if I consciously made the connection, but looking back now, I see that I faced a similar choice to what my father experienced: a decision whether to let a child come into the world or not. My father had chosen to abort a child because another baby would have been inconvenient for his doctoral studies. Would we now choose to terminate our son because he was not "normal"?

As prolife Christians, we realized, well, this is where we have to decide if we really mean what we believe. In the midst of long, tearful, and fearful conversations, we arrived at a simple conclusion: our default ethic should be to do no harm.

So we chose not to abort our child. But what would it mean to bring our son to term? What would it be like to raise a child with special needs? We had no idea.

We started reading books and resources about Down syndrome. We learned that about half of all babies with Down syndrome have heart conditions that require surgery. We read about the physical and mental challenges, the developmental delays, the need for early intervention and ongoing therapies. It was overwhelming. But we also learned that life with Down syndrome was not as scary as we had initially supposed. Because of better care and medical knowledge today, most people with Down syndrome can expect to have long and fruitful lives.

While I was learning about all this, it occurred to me that many children throughout history in various cultures around the world had been abandoned because of having special needs. Orphanages in China and many other countries continue to take in unwanted children, and there are never enough adoptive families to meet the need.

Historically, Christians were known for rescuing abandoned babies and raising them as their own. In the early centuries of the church, Christians practiced love and hospitality, welcoming little children into their homes who would otherwise not have survived. Others said of these Christians, "They alone know the right way to live." Their lives of compassion showed the world that God was real. Their love for the abandoned and marginalized was a concrete sign of God's love for all humanity.

Ellen and I realized that as the earliest Christians had, so we had a similar opportunity to demonstrate that same experience of God's love. If our son had been born in other circumstances, he may well have been one of those unloved, unwanted children. He could have been abandoned along the side of a road or thrown into a river to die. Come what may, regardless of whatever challenges were in store, we understood that welcoming our son was a God-given opportunity to practice the same kind of hospitality and love that Christians throughout the ages had been known for.

So we made a conscious choice to welcome our son with all love and care. While he was still in utero, we decided to name him so that he was not merely an abstract concept but a named, beloved son, a real person. So we gave him the name Elijah Timothy—Elijah being a Hebrew Old Testament name meaning "The Lord is God," and Timothy being a Greek New Testament name meaning "one who honors God." It was our prayer that his life would honor the Lord our God, and also that we and many others would learn to love and honor God through our son's life.

Elijah was born three weeks early on April 8, 2005. He spent several weeks in the neonatal intensive care unit as he adjusted to life on the outside. Many of the initial fears proved unfounded: he had no major organ defects, club feet, or cleft palate. A minor heart valve issue resolved on its own; and the only surgery he has needed was for ear tubes. Life has been a bit more complicated than usual with multiple doctors and therapists and whatnot, but nothing unmanageable. We now cannot imagine life without Elijah.

Elijah is now in elementary school, and while he has developmental delays and is smaller in stature than other classmates his age, he is doing remarkably well. He loves to read Curious George and Dora the Explorer books, and he is quite adept with his computer games and iPod apps. While he can be frustrating at times (aren't all kids?), he is also a delight and a blessing to all who encounter him.

I am grateful for the gift that God has given our family through our son Elijah. It is not exactly the life we had anticipated or expected, but it is a life of joy and blessing. As we grow in our love for him, we are delighted to see his love and affection for us. And if we mere mortals have such love for our special child, how much greater must God's immeasurable love be for us! Elijah's presence in our lives is a visible reminder that all life is sacred and that all of us are beloved by God.

≈

Being a father has helped me understand a little more about the fatherhood of God. When Josiah was a baby, I remember setting him on a counter in a church foyer. As he played on the counter, I hovered over him, ready to catch him if he should fall off the edge. And it occurred to me that perhaps God also hovers over me in ways that I cannot perceive or even imagine. I wish now that I could interact with my father as a fellow father and ask him what it was like for him when I was young, if he felt afraid or inadequate to the task of fatherhood. I am now older than the age he was when I was born, and it is funny to think of him as a young dad grappling with the challenges of parenting. What do any of us know, really?

All of us were damaged in some way by our parents, and we will inevitably mess up our own kids. That's just the way it is.[1] At the same time, we are also the recipients of various blessings from our parents, and by the grace of God, we may yet bring blessing to our own children.

In many ways I have defined my life in opposition to my father. I have consciously chosen to live differently from him, to show love and affection rather than distance and silence, to have faith rather than unbelief, to choose life rather than death. But on the other hand, I share with my father all the anxieties and inadequacies of fatherhood, and I find myself understanding more about our common humanity than I ever did when he was alive. So even though he is no longer with us, his memory is still very present with me and continues to shape me.

At his funeral, his co-workers told me that my dad was proud of me. I would like to think that he would be glad for the life I have lived in remembrance of him. Even though his own story was cut short, I would hope that he would see his life continuing on in his sons and grandsons in ways that bring honor and restoration to our family's story.

1. Craig Barnes writes, "We are as lost as our parents were. Someday our children will say the same." In *Yearning*.

6

Accepting Their Acceptability

ERIK KOLBELL

A Child of God?

It was Advent 1992, a bleak and slushy midwinter afternoon when my then-three-year-old daughter, Kate, was riding home from her parochial preschool on the back seat of my bicycle and regaling me with tales of all she had learned that day about the birth of the baby Jesus.

"He had a daddy named Joseph. And he had a mother named Mary," she said earnestly, then, after a pause, added, "And a sister named Toni." With seven years of biblical studies and twenty years of ministry under my belt, I thought I knew my way around the Nativity story pretty well, but I have to tell you, this was a new wrinkle for me. When later I tried to disabuse her of the idea that this first-century Semitic wonder boy born to a virgin had an elder sister likely of European extraction (Antoinette of Chartres? Tonya of Belgrade? Toni of Brooklyn?), Kate would have none of it, leaving me to conclude that if as she grew up her beliefs were not conventionally Christian they would at least be stubbornly held. And though to this day my now 21-year-old, agnosti-buddhist daughter no longer abides a belief in Toni, or, for that matter, the divinity of Jesus, she remains a young woman both committed to and guided by the principles to which she does abide. And that is fine with me.

It's fine with me in part because it speaks to a larger issue both of parenting and of faith, and that is the issue of acceptance vs. approval, or, in the theological vernacular, conditional vs. unconditional love. God does not just love us *because* of ourselves but often *despite* ourselves; does not love us *because* we tithe, or *because* we live by the same belief system as our parents, or *because*, every now and again, we turn the other cheek. Unconditional acceptance means that God loves us *despite* the pettiness that gets the better of our generosity, *despite* the impatience that trumps our serenity, *despite* the unease we sometimes feel when we come upon someone whose race or creed or tastes or politics or sexuality differs from our own. And this is good because this is grace. It is the thing Jesus felt for the harlots and tax collectors with whom he supped, and for the thief on the cross who asked for forgiveness: unmerited love, unearned forgiveness, unbidden mercy. And it is the thing that every child rightfully asks from every parent.

What they ask is that our love for them will not be jeopardized because they might, on occasion, make choices that differ from the ones we wish they'd made; and that however harshly—if justly—we might discipline them for misdeeds they should have known better than to commit, our love is not on the trading block. Our love is not for sale; it can't be bought with good grades in Sunday school or gold stars on a test paper any more than it can it be lost with bad manners, dubious body art, or missed curfews. It can't be heightened because our child makes a great play in the big game or lessened because she doesn't even want to play the game. It is an immutable truth that provides our children an immeasurable comfort.

As Elizabeth Barrett Browning so eloquently put it,

> If you love one another, let it be for love's sake only
>
> Do not say 'I love her for her smile, her look, her way of
>
> speaking gently or the trick of thought that agrees with me.'
>
> For these things in themselves may be changed.
>
> Or changed for you and love may be undone.

I don't want just to love my daughter because of her smile or her look or her "trick of thought." I also want to love her when the smile isn't there, when the look is scornful of me, and the trick of thought is one I vehemently disagree with.

Walking the Walk

It is all so much easier said than done, this notion of loving our children for who they are rather than for what we want them to be. I remember some years ago meeting with a couple who were expecting their first child, a son for whom I would be performing a baptism, and I used the conversation as an opportunity to tease out of them some of their thoughts on parenting. "We don't want to lay our values and expectations on our boy," the father told me, knowingly (if a little smugly). "We want him to find his beat, his rhythm, his tastes. We don't intend to put any judgments on him. If he wants to play baseball, great; if not, that's cool too. If he wants to play with dolls or become a vegetarian or paint his room day-glow purple, I'm fine with it."

"That's a wonderfully progressive outlook," I told them, and then asked, "Just curious; have you chosen a name for him yet?"

"Oh yeah," the dad chimed in. "Dylan. As in Bob Dylan. Any chance you could work a few lines of 'Subterranean Homesick Blues' into the baptism service?" I had to wonder how much equanimity Dad would muster if, a few years down the road, young Dylan's proclivity for, say, *Wayne Newton's Vegas Hits* trumped any interest he might show in "Like a Rolling Stone" or "A Hard Rain's A-Gonna Fall."

We don't necessarily want to "lay our values and expectations" onto our kids, but it's nearly impossible not to. Perhaps we name them after a saint (or rock star), or buy them Li'l Slugger pajamas. Perhaps we festoon their nursery with religious statuary, "Obama for President" stickers, or solemn posters about saving the seals. Our interests, our biases, our values and tastes become familiar to them both by osmosis and by exposure, and that's not necessarily a bad thing, especially if we believe in the integrity of those values. If, for instance, over the years I have demonstrated to my child that faith in God is important to me, then I hope she has drawn the conclusion that there is some inherent worth in asking herself what beliefs *she* holds dear, and why it might be important to live a truly examined life.

The danger comes when we—either subtly or not—convey to our children how much more highly their stock will rise in our eyes if their views are in sync with ours, or that our love for them is commensurate with the compatibility of our beliefs. That, then, becomes love *because*. It is Browning's "loving her for her smile, her look, her way of speaking gently," which is no love at all. I would rather that my child find her own "way of speaking gently," her own voice, even if it be notably different from mine in tone and timbre, than to mimic the one she thinks I want to hear simply because it will be pleasing to me.

Tastes are One Thing, Morals Another

This business of *love despite* is difficult enough to pull off when our kids diverge from us on relatively benign issues such as taste or style or interests. Many a parent's endeavor to practice unconditional acceptance can find itself sorely tested when her thirteen-year-old daughter's hairstyle goes from Prom Queen French Curl to Multi-Spiked Rainbow-Punk, much the same way many other parents might find themselves swallowing their disappointment when the son they were keeping a seat warm for in the venerable family law firm has decided instead that his fortune lies in the distinctly riskier and less conventional field of, say, circus performance. But we can juggle these discrepancies between our hopes and their dreams when we muster up sufficient maturity to remind ourselves that if happiness is the destination, there are many different roads to take us there.

What's trickier is the business of loving our kids when the choices they're making are not only foreign to us but destructive to them, bending away not only from conventional norm but from moral acceptability. What does love look like when it's directed to a child who has been caught lying to her parents, cheating on an exam, or bullying some poor kid out of his lunch money? Do we become parental pushovers who adopt a recklessly hands-off policy with regard to discipline and punishment? Or do we find a way to hate the sin and love the sinner, all the while mindful of the fact that it is in *our* proclivity to sin that we find our capacity to forgive. The answer, I think, is best illustrated by a story I was once privy to.

Some years ago, late one night I found myself at the police headquarters of a small New England city. I was there to help a college student who had gotten himself in some minor trouble, and in the waiting lounge was the single mother of a young man who, as she explained, had been picked up with some buddies for stealing a car and taking it for a joyride. When the boy was brought out of his cell and into the lounge, he had a look on his face I could only describe as confused defiance. I don't think he knew what to make of the situation, what possessed him to do what he did, or how his mom was going to manage things. He looked emotionally guarded, perhaps ready at a moment's notice to justify his act as a youthful prank or a dare gone bad, or perhaps to fall on the mercy of his mother's softer side. It's what happened next that made things clear for him.

His mother looked him sternly in the eye and said to him in a strong but quavering voice, "Son, I love you. And I am so brokenhearted and so angry at what you did." The boy wept, the mom wept. Even the grizzled desk sergeant looked a little teary. The two embraced, holding each other tight, as if by letting go they would spin into separate universes of alienation and recrimination from which they might never recover. And then they went home.

What I found so powerful was that the mother expressed both of her paradoxical sentiments with equal conviction, and they were received with equal certainty. Her love of this boy and her fury over his actions were held in identical measure. It was Mom's way of saying, "Look, as a parent, my devotion to you is rock-solid, immutable, and without reservation. But a part of that parental devotion involves doing whatever I deem fit to mold you into a good person who understands right from wrong and is willing to be held accountable for the consequences of bad decisions."

When I think of this little slice of life, I'm reminded in the Gospel according to John of the unnamed woman picked up by the Pharisees, who intend to stone her for her infidelity. (One wonders if they held the man with whom she was unfaithful in similar judgment, but that's grist for another discussion altogether.) Jesus intervenes on her behalf, challenges the sinless in the mob to cast the first stone (none do, of course), refuses to condemn the woman himself, and then sends her on her way with the admonition, "Now go, and sin no more." He saved her life in two ways, I think. By preventing the stoning he saved her mortal life but by telling her to leave her life of sin he saved her soul the same way the mother sought to save her son's soul, by molding her into a good person who feels worthy of forgiveness and is then willing to live a life reflective of that worthiness.

So, is unconditional love at odds with disciplined parenting and a desire to point your child's moral compass in the right direction? I don't think so, not if the mixture of the two can compel our kids to "go and sin no more," or at least to chart a wise and ethical course for their lives. And with that in mind I would offer you five brief guidelines for exercising that discipline.

Disciplined Parenting Guidelines

1. Make a Distinction

When you're calling your child to task for a disciplinary lapse, keep in mind that there is a difference between who we are and what we do. I once saw a young boy of about eleven picking on a schoolmate who was clearly weaker and meeker than he. In a heartbeat the children's teacher descended on the boy, held him firmly by the arms, made eye contact, and said to him "Jackie, you're a smart kid doing a really, really stupid thing." How the teacher managed the situation from then on is beside my point, which is that she began by separating the trouble-making boy's sense of who he is (". . . you're a smart kid . . .") from what he did (". . . a really, really stupid thing.")

Theologically this is a critical distinction because as Christians we believe we are cast in God's image ("fearfully and wonderfully made," is how the psalmist put it), so to condemn who we are is to reject the essential goodness with which God infuses us. But it is also a critical psychological distinction because it's more within a child's reach to be able to change what he does than to change who he is (or who he has come to believe he is); behavior is more malleable than self-image, and the more a child hears things like "you're stupid," "you're bad," or "you're clumsy," the more ingrained that message becomes, until it so thoroughly internalized that it is almost impossible to uproot.

2. Be Age Appropriate

I remember watching the mother of a three-year-old boy discussing the evening's itinerary with the child. "First we'll have dinner, okay? And then, after dinner, I want you to take a bath, okay? And then, how about if we put on your pajamas?" And so the conversation went.

What drove me nuts about this little scene was the mother's insistent "okay?" That was tantamount to asking the child's permission to feed and bathe him. The smaller the child, the larger the world looks; and the larger the world looks, the more they need us to call the shots, set the boundaries, and draw the limits. I think it's a real temptation, under the guise of giving our toddlers a sense of responsibility, to burden them with freedom. Little kids don't want to negotiate every last detail of life, they want to find comfort in the knowledge that if we're having them do something, it's because we know it is better that they do it than that they don't. Love, as St. Paul taught us, is patient and kind; it does not envy or boast. It is also, at times, restrictive, even dictatorial. This is why the Ten Commandments were not the Ten Suggestions.

The freedom to make our own decisions must unfold gradually for us, over time and circumstance. Children innately understand that this is how they want it to happen, and in some primitive fashion understand that it is for their own good. A three-year-old doesn't need to decide when or what he should eat for dinner; a seven-year-old doesn't need to be confronted with the ethical ambiguities that come with sexual activity; a twelve-year -old doesn't need the keys to the car; and a seventeen-year-old doesn't need the freedom to stay out all hours on a school night and not account for her whereabouts. Granting these kinds of latitude is less an expression of enlightened liberalism and more of malign neglect. Unconditional love, on the other hand, is made manifest in these circumstances when we make the child's world small enough and safe enough that we ensure their own sense of security.

3. Play Fair

Be fair with your children, establish clear boundaries with them, and enforce those boundaries with consistency. Here's another story to illustrate my point:

When Kate was about seven years old, she was at Daniel's house for an after-school playdate. I told her ahead of time that I would be by to pick her up at 6:00, after which she and I would go home and have our Tuesday evening ritual dinner of pizza and ice cream (father-daughter night; my wife worked late on Tuesdays).

When I got to the apartment where Daniel's family lived, Kate and Daniel were watching a video, so I went over to Kate, told her that it would be 6:00 in ten minutes, that I would tell her when it *was* 6:00, and that *if* she then put on her coat and picked up her school things as we agreed, we would indeed have our pizza supper. Daniel's mother then said to me, "They're pretty into this video, so what're you gonna do if she doesn't come when you call her?"

"If she doesn't come when I call her," I told the mom, "if she ignores me, we'll just have something a whole lot more pedestrian for dinner."

"You mean you'll actually follow through on your veiled threat?" she asked incredulously.

"Well," I answered, "you can look at it as a threat or you could look at it as a transaction for which we both hold some responsibility."

Now, I don't tell you this story to make myself out to be a paragon of perfect parenting; the mistakes I've made over the years could fill more pages than I have been allotted here. But I did see this as a useful opportunity to make the point to Daniel's mom that if we're reasonable with our children, if we're clear with them, and if we consistently do what we say we'll do as a consequence either of their obedience or disobedience, then we're loving them in a way that provides them with an immeasurable sense of both security and justice.

4. Do as I Do

This is self-evident to the point of being nearly unnecessary to mention, but our kids are pretty finely attuned to how we parents comport ourselves, which means that when there's a disparity, they're much more likely to absorb the ethics we practice than the ethics we preach. If we teach them to be generous while we're stepping over the beggar in the street, or counsel them patience just after we've railed about the traffic jam we're stuck in we can probably count on them to grow up to be a little less sensitive and a little more short-fused than we'd like them to be.

5. Give Yourself a Break

Finally, let's all remember that just as our kids are learning how to grow up, we, too, are new to the job of parenting. We don't have all the answers and can benefit as much from love and forgiveness as our sons and daughters can. We do well to go a little easy on ourselves, love ourselves despite *our* shortcomings, by remembering that parenting is a learn-on-the-job process. The old saying goes that when something bad happens, we can either fix the problem or we can fix the blame, and while I've never known anyone whose learned much from their mistakes when they're driven to harbor the blame, I do know an awful lot of people—young and old—who have benefited mightily when they've looked back at those mistakes or the mistakes of others and said simply, "Okay, what has this taught us?"

To Love for Love's Sake

It's an old adage that through God's grace forgiveness trumps imperfection. Apropos of parenting, we don't have to be perfect if we are forgiving of ourselves, just as our kids don't have to be perfect if we are forgiving of them. Mistakes made by either generation are teaching moments, redeemed not by punishment for punishment's sake, but by love and wisdom seasoned with discipline and justice. When we as parents screw up on the job it's alright to give ourselves a second chance, so that the lazy parent learns to be diligent, the reactionary parent patient, the hypocritical parent principled. Likewise, when we meet our children's foibles with the same kind of forgiving love similar results can ensue. The belligerent youth becomes accepting, the impertinent one respectful, the selfish one benevolent. Not overnight, of course, but a consistent outpouring of loving mercy can act like water run smooth over hard granite, wearing down even the most stubborn stone and doing so slowly, gradually, but persistently.

I suspect this is the kind of upbringing Jesus himself received, for how else would it have come to be revealed in his teaching, let alone his comportment. Heck, I wouldn't be surprised if it was the kind of upbringing Toni received as well.

7

Sister, Daughter, Friend

RODNEY R. CLAPP

EVERYONE IS AN EXPERT on parenting—until he or she has a child. Then we find ourselves cast into a land of mysteries and wonders, and not a few complications. I like best the metaphor of the parent as anthropologist. A child lives in a strange, foreign land, with a language parents must learn, and a set of fears and hopes not always easy for a parent, a grownup, to interpret. Take for instance the frequent toddler fear of being washed down the drain of the bathtub. The thoughtless parent may scoff and even (mildly, we hope) mock his child's fright. But the thoughtful parent, the parent as anthropologist, will reflect that the child watches all the water wash away and down around her, and just moments before the body of water was bigger than the child. If the water can be sucked down the drain, why not the child? It takes awhile for the toddler to understand that the water's body is a different sort of body than her own, and that her own, more solid body, is impervious to the sucking horrors of the drain.

My wife and I were drawn into the mysterious land of the child by our only child, a daughter, Jesselyn. Like other parents, we were not fully prepared for parenthood. Educated and bookish, we had read our share of manuals. We had and frequently continued consulting our parents, who had ushered us through the strange land of childhood and could speak with the authority of experience.

But Sandy and I were (and are) Christians, so we had another source of authority for our guidance into parenthood. We looked to the church.

What the church told us about our relationship with our child gave us the animating principle for our parenting. Or, rather, we might say it was not only what the church told us that supremely guided us, but what the church did to our child.

And what the church did to our child was baptize her. Baptism meant that Jesselyn was not only *our* child, but the church's child. In baptism, the Apostle Paul says, all Christians are made first and foremost siblings to one another. So we took seriously the reality that Jesselyn was first our sister in Christ, and only second our daughter in the flesh.

This animating principle meant that our highest responsibility to our daughter was to raise her in the faith, and to do so with the assistance of the church. We then turned often, and thankfully, to Jesselyn's godparents. One godparent especially was a constantly available babysitter, adviser, and encourager. She walked with us through the various stages of Jesselyn's childhood, and especially her babyhood and toddlerhood, where she needed constant attention. The extent of this godparent's patience sometimes became apparent retrospectively, after we had passed through a particular stage and the godparent later confessed that a stage required abundant patience. So, for example, the stage of parental infatuation was one where the godparent would visit our apartment. For an hour or two before bedtime we would play with and feed and obsess over the baby. Then, after we put her to bed, we dragged out videotapes, showing another hour or so of Jesselyn crawling, banging pots and pans, crying, smiling, cooing in the bath. It took commitment to sit through so many sessions of a couple's infatuation and obsessiveness with their baby, and this godparent gave the gift of her patience.

Taking baptism as the animating principle of our parenting meant something in addition to asking the church (especially in the form of a godparent) to walk alongside us for the adventure of parenting. It meant that, from early on, we anticipated our daughter's own, mature discipleship. Of course, it was necessary that we treat her as a child, a dependent. But we looked ahead to when she would say her own prayers, and grow up into her own degree of independence. Eventually, God willing, she would become a grown sister in baptism, a mature friend in Christ.

We knew that adolescence, at least, would bring tougher, more challenging days of parenthood. Then Jesselyn would be more on her own, more out of our constant purview. Looking back, I now see that we intuitively built what I would now call "parental capital" with our child. We introduced her to our enthusiasms—music, books, movies, and animals—and hoped that she would grow into these endeavors as we had grown into them and as we continued to grow into them long after we had first become adults. Then, after adolescence and beyond, we would still have much to share with her, in life and in faith.

So from her earliest days Jesselyn heard not only the children's singer Raffi, but Elvis and John Coltrane. We sang with her not only nursery songs, but (in the church's gathered worship) the great hymns of the faith. When Jesselyn was ten, our bedtime reading was Tolkien's *The Hobbit*. We insisted (though with more constancy than success) that she feed and water and help care for the family dog.

Then, when Jesselyn reached her early teens, we faced the question of how to deal with the more mature media of our hypermediated culture. What about movies and songs with violence, graphic sexuality, and other mature themes? Somehow I hit on a simple but highly effective idea. Jesselyn would not simply be restricted from, say, PG-13-rated films. But if she were to see a questionable movie, she would have to see it with her father, and then discuss it afterwards.

The teenaged aversion to anything remotely resembling parental lectures weeded out many movies. Jesselyn would simply decide it wasn't worth the trouble. But in other cases she really wanted to view a given movie, so we would go together, then afterwards talk about the characters, their motivations, the happenings of the plot, and how all these things reflected or did not reflect family and Christian values. So she better learned, I think, to be a judicious viewer and listener and reader. And in the process I gained a friend, a daughter now aged twenty-three who makes her own movie, music, and other recommendations, and who often guides me in better enjoying and understanding them.

Reading back over what I've here written, it strikes me that I've painted too rosy a picture. Our church is called St. Barnabas, and it shows how much popular culture penetrated our young daughter's conscience that when, asked at age four where she went to church, she answered, "St. Barnes and Noble." And it was only many years later that she admitted that *The Hobbit*'s Gollum gave her nightmares, casting a shadow on my choice to read it to her when she was so young, and believing her ten-year-old protestations that the book did not give her nightmares.

All said, however, we have been extraordinarily lucky or blessed or both. For today we have a mature, levelheaded and keenly observant daughter, a sister in the faith, and a friend in the enjoyment of many of our most rewarding passions.

8

The Heritage of Story

DALE BROWN

My father laughingly says that he was "jerked up by the hair of his head." That's how he describes his upbringing. Next to youngest in a family of thirteen, he went to the Tennessee fields early, made it through eighth grade in the one-room schoolhouse on Dry Creek, and fled the farm at sixteen. On twenty-five dollars borrowed from his sister, my Aunt Kate, he hitch-hiked his way north to a tomato-canning factory in Tipton, Indiana. After a stint overseas during World War II, he came back to Middle America to a factory job and a 1950s routine that would open the worlds of libraries, televisions, colleges, and more to me.

What Dad had learned about parenting involved a belt and a stern word. I do not recall anyone ever using the word *parenting* in the 1950s. I am confident that fatherhood seminars, how-to classes, and parent-training symposia came along much later. My father was on his own with little more than the example of his own father, Napoleon Francis Brown, or Poli, as he was known along the creek. They never had electricity or "indoor plumb-ing" (a euphemism for the outhouse—or the privy, as they would say down home). Up north, they had lights and bathrooms and more.

Nobody used the words *migration* or *displacement* in 1949, the year I was born. Families like mine learned all sorts of new terms: *white trash*, *hillbilly*, *hick*, *redneck*, and *cracker*—in Indiana and Michigan and Ohio. Nevertheless, after the war, my father tried hard to fit in so far from home, so far from Dry Creek. He laughed when the guys at Delco-Remy asked him if his wife was wearing shoes yet. He rubbed the edges off his hill country accent.

My father wanted desperately to overcome the poverty and sense of inferiority that he'd packed along from the Creek. I think he suspected that the way ahead was somehow related to education and church. He read Dale Carnegie in the fifties. Once I happened in on a meeting in our basement where Dad and two of his fellow Carnegie class members had gathered around a wash tub. They had rolled up newspapers with which they were pounding that rickety tub. "I'm coming out of this shell," they were shouting.

My dad had plans for beating the system. He didn't know anything about basketball, for example, but he knew every Indiana boy played that game. So he got a discarded light pole from one of his cousins who worked for the power company, built a huge backboard from lumber he had in the garage, and stuck the whole thing, painted white, in a hole in the yard. It must have been twelve feet high and the grass soon gave way to constant mud. I dribbled months of my childhood away out there.

Sitting out behind the garage with our ratty-eared dog running underfoot, Dad told me about learning to talk their way. He told me about laughing along with the jokesters and their jibes about having a toilet inside the house and such. But the battle he was fighting was for me. I see that now. I'm sure he was homesick for that creek he'd fled. The creek was too deep in him to ever truly leave behind. He all but told me that day out by the light pole basketball contraption. Looking over at our spaniel, he said, "That there pup fancies himself a bird dog, but all his fancyin' it don't make it so." That became a line to remember.

The factory job, however, paved the way into the middle class. Someone should say thank you to General Motors. For my twelfth birthday, Dad brought home a Standard Transistor Radio with two shortwave bands. In fifties turquoise, the battery-powered machine was expensive—$50.00 at Decker's store. And it opened up worlds. Late into the night I would listen to foreign voices jabbering on KMOX in Saint Louis or WLS in Chicago. I could only imagine.

Never a bookish man except for that one book, the Bible, Dad nonetheless knew that books tied into this climbing business. Every Saturday morning for me was the YMCA and the Carnegie Library, both marvelous places. At the library they let you pick out six books for free. It amazed me every time, just like the magic dial of the radio in the dark bedroom.

When all the kids were buying car coats, Dad made sure I got one, a splendid maroon with a hood and oversized pockets. It cost $75.00 at Surbaugh's downtown. I often wonder what became of that coat. I think that was the only time we ever went to Surbaugh's. We were mostly K-Mart and J.C. Penney folks.

I was, therefore, my father's investment in the future. He worked at it like a convict pounding rocks, and I was no easy project. When I was ten or so, he'd bought me a used .410 shotgun and took me hunting along the creek on one of our frequent trips to the home place in Tennessee. After being carefully instructed in the requisite safety procedures, I managed to fire the gun accidentally. Pieces of shale from the dry creek bed flew into my father's face.

When I was sixteen, he tried to teach me about the cars he had learned to tinker with since his removal to the Midwest. I jacked up the old Bel-Aire in the driveway. Having taken the wheel off, Dad was turning the drum when the car plummeted off the jack. My fouled-up jacking job caused permanent damage to his hand. Nowadays he shakes hands left-handed because of me and his crippled right hand.

What do you do with a kid like that? Forgive him. Dad never brings that stuff up. He kept on telling the stories, however: the ones I can still get lost in—Dry Creek and a factory town up Highway 31-E. Grandpa Poli slept with a pistol under his pillow. Dad kept a shotgun in the closet. I keep a baseball bat beside the bed. Some change, I guess. When my own children came along, I tried to talk with them like my dad had talked to me. And forgive them, too. They grew up on Poli's stories and Dad's mixed and jumbled with some of my own.

Dad always talked to me at Fred Farlow's barbershop on 29th Street. It was a real man kind of place—girlie posters and ballgame chatter, guys who said damn and had tattoos. Given the hint of the dentist's chair in the barber's one, I always felt fidgety when it was my turn on the little red bench Mister Farlow put across the arms of the chair. I'd try to make my neck big so the apron wouldn't be too tight around my neck. Mr. Farlow would give me bubble gum, and Dad would buy me a Coke in a nickel bottle. While we waited, Dad would ask about school and wonder if I was fitting in.

We'd talk on the way to church or when he was out doing odd jobs at Mrs. Darlington's big house or at the Anderson Memorial Park, a grave-yard where he mowed around the stones and monuments of people with regular names like Miller and Gray. Somehow being with Dad there in the graveyard was like being back at Turkey Town on a hill near Dry Creek, where we went every July to see the kinfolk and deck out the graves with plastic flowers. When he'd take a break, we'd read people's lives in the stones they'd had put up. "Elizabeth Miller—Beloved Of Her Children." "Robert Gray—Loving Father." Sometimes we'd see a stone for a kid who'd died with plots beside it for the parents who weren't there yet. I wondered how that would feel. Dad would point out how young some of them had been when they died. And he'd shake his head.

I collected lots of his stories in the car going back and forth to those odd jobs, but I heard even more in the winter after school, before supper, because we had no television set in those days, and I couldn't play ball against the cold wind. Other times I'd sit and listen to the Sunday dinner talk when some folks from church were there, and they'd all be talking about the old days and forget about me. "Why don't you go on out and play now?" Mom would suggest, but I'd generally hang around and hear most of it. Now I'm glad for that, because those overheard reminiscences became the path toward knowing something of my folks—maybe a way toward knowing myself as well.

"When I first got married and went to Indiana," Dad said, "I wanted real bad to hunker down and fit in there. I remember going shopping at the Payless with your mom. We'd buy stuff we saw other people buying. We even bought some frozen biscuits once, 'spite the fact that we didn't have no freezer. We laid 'em on the window ledge till they finally swole up and exploded. Then we'd laugh about how silly we was." Dad had lots of stories like that one. Turning the empty feeling into humor was a way of coping with being on the outside of the jokes or not knowing the right people and the right neighborhoods, the right habits and local rituals.

Southerners going North in the 40s and 50s often clustered in little colonies of friends and neighbors—a bulwark against other colonies—Black folks on one side of the tracks, Polish Catholics on the other, rich folks in Edgewood, and solid Yankee folks in Meadowbrook. The southerners got used to the jokes. You know the one about the Reb tied to a stake in heaven? The visitor asks Saint Peter why that man is tied up that way. Saint Peter says, "Why he's from Tennessee. If we don't tie him up, he'll go home."

So the hillbillies learned to smile and find their own. The segregation became most obvious on Sundays at 10:00. Southern churches like the Church of Christ began to pop up everywhere in northern cities by the late 40s, little clubs where southerners could minister to their own. And here my mom and dad found a familiar scent, southern transplants like themselves at the Madison Avenue Church of Christ. Serious-minded men with enough accent left to be identifiable as Pike County or Overton County told them how to handle this money they were making, and how to raise their kids, and how God was looking over their shoulders. Solemnness settled in on these newcomers who had found the pot of gold in the north.

I grew up in that church as much as I grew up in my own family: Sunday morning worship and Sunday school, Sunday night singing, Monday night prayer meeting, Wednesday night Bible study, Thursday night visitation, Saturday night chili supper. Then we'd do it again.

Madison Avenue Church of Christ gathered in a brown shingled building meant to look like brick. We had a tiny vestibule and a big room of pews—enough for 150 people or so, though I never saw it full. The basement, damp and concretey, was for Sunday school classes and strict Bible lessons to balance out our public schools, despite the fact that, in those early 50s, they had a good bit of the Bible about them too. "We wanted the best for you and your sister," Dad tells me. "We always hauled you to church—twice on Sundays and Wednesday nights, all the revivals and special services; we changed your diapers on the back pews and prayed for you to get baptized 'cause we believed that was the way home." The church was a passport to meaning, so we all plunged in.

Talking about his own conversion, Dad says he "went forward that night scared to death." I already knew enough to know what he was telling me, because I'd trembled too under the strong words about hell. I had my own going forward ahead of me yet. Mom wrote down what he said that night just weeks after I was born. She's showed it to me many times on a scrap of paper she keeps in her Bible. "My life isn't what I want his to be," he said. And he pointed at me. Now there's something to live up to, huh?

But it wasn't only going to church; it was *being* the church as Dad would say it. He tried to give good examples. Once when we were at one of his odd jobs—covering up the dirty walls in one of our local real-estate tycoon's run-down rentals. A down-and-out looking guy came in and asked for a handout. Dad was smearing on the white paint while I got in the way, but I remember him putting down the roller he'd screwed on to the end of a stick to do the ceilings with and wiping off his hands and digging all the money he had out of his spattered pants. Eighty-five cents this time. The scraggly fellow said thanks and tottered along. I thought about the baseball cards I could have bought with even half of those eighty-five cents.

Another time I recall Mom and Dad taking in a woman and her three kids. The kids played with my sister and me while their mom was out looking for work. Suddenly one afternoon, a wild man showed up at the door. He shouted at Dad, and I was scared. "Well, what'd you think you were doing," the man yelled. But Dad stood right up to him. "Just helpin' out," Dad said. Finally, when the man calmed down, we found out he was the father of those three kids, and his wife had found work all right. He'd come in from Kentucky to find her working in the hotel rooms on the north side. Mom shooed me out of the room about then. But my folks were serious about carrying the gospel "to every creature."

I still have the Bible he marked up there in the bathroom on Saturday nights. Antique Bibles can be like fantastic archeological finds. He always had Mom do whatever writing needed to be done around the house—signing report cards and writing checks. I think he was embarrassed about his scrawl. But the thin leaves of his Bible ran blue and black with smeared underlinings and notes, mostly unreadable to anyone but him, and the pages were worn nearly through with the handling. It's full of pieces clipped from church bulletins and programs of assignments for doing communion and leading prayers and such. I like to keep it around. That falling-apart Bible summarizes the devotion of those early Indiana years. He knocked on doors to invite strangers to church; he fought back his horrible fears to actually stand up front and give a brief talk from Scripture. He took part in the business meetings, and finally became a leader of the flock. He found a place to belong.

And such became my inheritance. I have handed on these stories to my children and added a few of my own. My stories haven't the same edge as those of my father. When he was a kid, some boys down the creek killed their father with a ball peen hammer. I could tell my kids about the time the steering wheel came off in my hand when I was driving the old bus carrying the singing group I was part of. Some drama, but far from the same degree.

One of the tragedies of parenting, I suppose, is that you can never really explain your younger self to your children. Even old yearbooks and home movies, yellowing photographs and the battered transistor radio you've held onto cannot adequately capture the stuff bubbling in your heart before they were born. I have no way of peering into the reality of my father, the ten-year-old boy who cut off his toe with an accidental mis-hit of the axe while chopping wood. I have little sense of the young man who sold his 1948 Ford when I was born, so he could make a downpayment on a house for me to start out in. And I can only imagine the courage it took to come out of that shell on the way North from Dry Creek. But I can imagine. I have the stories.

My children know a little about my working in the K-Mart during college, my decision to leave school for five years, the flailing attempts at ministry, the teaching career, that year in Wales, and the struggles to find a place. But how can I convey to them the Vietnam nervousness, the work in inner-city St. Louis, the snowstorm where I fell in love with their mother, that traveling troupe, the struggles with faith and doubt? Family reunions rarely get that far past the weather, the ballgame, or the latest sensation on the cable news networks. Our ubiquitous media has endangered us by giving us all the same story, I suppose.

But my kids have some stories of their own to get them part of the way. My father has Dry Creek deep in him. I have Madison Avenue Church of Christ deep in me. The kids will have to get by on that. They are mostly grown now and respectful when the stories flow out. There's something there for them, and I think they suspect so in their best moments.

These stories reveal character. They tell you about someone's history, of course; but, more than that, they tell you about what has carried meaning for that person. It all comes down to metaphor, I suppose. What I have learned from my father is to look for the meanings deep within events, the story within the stories. Looking back, he sees the hand of a good God in the circumstances of his life. I've spent most of a lifetime listening for that wind of providence.

In my father's story, any listener would hear echoes of the American dream crisscrossed by a preoccupation with the life of faith. My mother is a Martha, and the first Bible verse I remember hearing was "Martha, Martha, thou art cumbered about with many things." My father laughingly kept that passage circulating in our family circle. In that Mary and Martha story, Christ approves of Mary because she has chosen "the one essential." My father was after that, and that was no joking matter. His earnestness is *the* family story.

His stories and mine meet at that intersection of trying to find what matters ultimately. My children will one day tell the stories of my past, some they were in on, some they've only heard. I can only hope that those tales lead them toward something essential.

We have parenting classes now, of course, and how-to books, and advice on the Internet; but I wonder if we really know how the whole business works? My father didn't know what he was doing. Nor do I. But the stories are good ones, eh? At the end of the day, we both hope that the stories will be enough. My father's longing when he left the hills, and my longing when I left the Middle West are all a piece of the same longing, I suspect. And all longing, one hopes, is a longing for God.

9

On Being a Stepfather

M. CRAIG BARNES

I am a stepfather. But I cannot write on behalf of all stepfathers because we who bear this label wear it differently.

Stepfathers of young children have a different experience from those who enter the family when the children are older. Stepfathers who bring their own children into the family deal with different issues from those who do not. And those who marry widows encounter very different dynamics from those who marry divorced women.

The various ways of being a stepfather are also shaped by the diverse personalities within a new family undergoing significant transition. A family is changed when even a dog is brought into the house. Bringing in a new man, and possibly his children, disrupts the balance of the prior family. Reactions inevitably follow. And everyone's identity and role in the new family is shaped by the particular reactivity of everyone else.

All these diverse dynamics make it necessary to treat each blended family as unique. Thus, prescriptions for a particular way to be a stepfather are often irrelevant. Since it's impossible to do justice to all of the ways of stepparenting in a brief chapter, I have chosen simply to present my own experience.

I was divorced after a long marriage. Eventually, I met and married a divorced woman named Dawne, who has two sons. At the time of our wedding her boys were nine and seven years old. For over five years we've lived together as a family.

I have a daughter who was in her twenties when my first marriage came to an end. She is now living in a different state and raising a family of her own. She was a great support to both of her parents when we were divorcing, and we remain as close as you can be when you live far away. Dawne frequently sends her mother-to-mother care packages, and they get along well, but my daughter doesn't perceive her as a stepmother. She is happy that we're happy. But it would stretch the term *blended family* to say that she blended into the family created by my second marriage.

The term *blended family* more appropriately applies to the experiences that began after I moved into the home Dawne formerly shared with her young boys and took on the role of stepfather. These are some of the dynamics we experience.

Falling in Love

Dawne and I took the risk of exchanging vows only because we believe that two people who have failed at previous marital commitments could be forgiven of their sins, healed of their hurts, rescued from their guilt, and freed to make a new commitment. All of that happened only by the mercy of God. Grace is not just a concept for us. It is what God's love has so clearly done in our lives, and these days we are better at allowing this love to flow out of our lives into those around us.

When Dawne and I were preparing to marry, the topic we discussed the most was how it would impact her sons. We consulted therapists, friends who had already navigated these waters, and probably too much professional literature. I am a veteran pastor of a local congregation and a seminary professor. Dawne has a degree in social work. We thought we had a pretty good idea of the dynamics we were about to confront. What we had not accounted for was that her sons and I would also fall in love. That is what allows us to navigate our issues.

They don't actually feel like issues to us. It just feels like another family that trusts in love and believes it creates the opportunity, even calling, to work through whatever is before us. When we clumsily stumble into problems associated with merging two different ways of life, like the unimportant but nagging issue of whether a coat should be hung up or draped over a chair, it's the love that makes us careful with each other. And it makes us quick to forgive and even grin over the different styles of being at home. But after five years it still doesn't come automatically. All four of us have learned to step back, take a moment, and let the love determine our responses. At least, that's true in our best moments.

Love isn't only something that is given; it's also received, and believed. It is because I trust their love that I refuse to believe I am in the way of the family patterns the three had developed long before I arrived. Blessedly, all three of them give me daily reasons to believe I am a cherished member of our family. Nothing about this is natural for any family. By nature, we resist change. So in a blended family it takes more conscious effort to trust in the love. Stepfathers are not given the luxury of resting upon biological ties that have existed as long as the children have been alive.

This is not unlike the dynamic between God's grace and our faith. It is not enough that God promises to be faithful in loving us unconditionally. Unless we have faith in that grace, we cannot really enjoy the relationship. In our blended family, that means we choose to trust affirmations of love over whatever feelings of marginalization may emerge in the course of a bad day. The boys and I keep choosing to believe that we are not in each other's way of loving Dawne. We have faith in the gracious commitment we all made to each to other that we are a family. But again, that involves daily choices to believe in our beliefs.

Three Plus One

The Apostle Paul was quite devoted to ensuring that Gentiles were accepted into the church that was once composed only of Jewish Christians. The fact that he had to work so hard on this issue demonstrates how difficult it is to incorporate the stranger into an existing community. And a family is a community. In our family I am tempted to keep thinking of myself as the Gentile.

Dawne and her two boys were solidified as a family of three long before I showed up. So it was unreasonable for me to assume that the three of them would easily become the four of us. But the irrationality didn't prevent me from assuming it. When we were married I thought that the former ways Dawne and the boys had been a family would disappear, and the four of us would build new ways. Not only was that naïve and dishonoring, but it also doesn't make theological sense. The arrival of Gentiles into the church changed its character, but they didn't throw out all of the Jewish traditions. This is why the church has an Old Testament. Similarly, my arrival into the home of a family of three cannot and should not mean that they forget about all of their formative years together and start over with me. While it's true that after I arrived all four of us made dramatic changes, these were changes to an ongoing family system.

I now realize that the three-plus-one issue will never fully go away. Some days I deal well with it, which means ignoring it, but most days present some little reminder that I am at best the beloved stepfather. Being beloved is amazing. The boys love me as their stepfather who came to the party late. Their primal years were spent having their needs met solely through their mother. To this day, there are times when one of the boys will make a phone call to his mother for help even though I'm seated ten feet away from him. Dawne will typically tell them to ask me, and they're happy to do that. They aren't ignoring me. It just doesn't occur to them to think of me as a parent who can help them line up a playdate.

It is also significant that no matter how much I want to fantasize about being the boys' father, for their sake I need to think of myself as a stepfather. They have a father who is involved in their lives. No child grows up well with confusion about these primary parental identities.

Given these limitations, we are still very much a cohesive family. We live under the same roof, eat and play together, share household chores, discuss values, say "I love you" often through the day, take turns saying the blessing as we hold hands at the table, and cuddle together as a foursome on a large couch in front of the TV. So it's best not to make too much of this three-plus-one dynamic, but it frequently emerges in my mind. As much as this disturbs me, it probably creates more stress for Dawne, who often feels caught in the middle of this subtle tension. She loves to be needed by her sons. But she also is constantly trying to draw me into their threesome. It is hard to blend a fourth into a group of three.

It doesn't help that I am by nature an introvert and often fret about being in the way. Since I always have plenty of work to do, it's tempting for me to retire to the home study where I feel needed. I have to ask myself constantly if the time wouldn't be better used sitting on that couch with them in front of a television show that I really don't care about. That is also where I am needed.

The boys easily take direction from me as one of the leaders of the family, but I have to be careful not to speak sternly because it devastates them. Even my simple reminder to do their homework can send them in the ditch. By contrast when their mother disciplines the boys, they take it in stride. The three of them can argue and laugh together within a five-minute span. Dawne believes they overreact to my correction because they want so much to please me. It feels like that. So clearly the three plus one dynamic doesn't mean I'm unimportant. Ironically, it means that as a stepfather I have more ability to do damage than I ever did as a father. And thus my need to be always careful with them also creates some distance. I would quickly trade such odd power for a more normal parental role in their lives, but this is our normal. As a result, I offer plenty of leadership to the boys in ordinary matters, but if I have a discipline concern I take it up with their mother.

Having raised a daughter in my first marriage, I thought I knew about parenting. But I'm now helping a mother raise her sons. We typically refer to the boys as our sons, but this is a gracious allusion to my love and shared responsibility in raising them. "Our sons" masks the reality that I've entered an ongoing family. It's amazing how steep the learning curve has been for me, not only because of the gender differences between daughters and sons, but more significantly because this time I'm the stepfather.

Naming

Our biblical tradition affirms that naming is important. Not only is God's character revealed in such names as Yahweh, Elohim, El Shaddai, Emmanuel, and Savior, but so are humans often given new names when they discover their new mission. Abram becomes Abraham, Sari become Sarah, Cephas becomes Peter, and Saul becomes Paul the Apostle. Becoming a stepfather also means taking on a new mission, and so it is good to think about the name the children should call him.

"Dad" didn't seem right to us since the boys already had a father whom they see once a week, and their mother and I wanted to honor that relationship. But we didn't think it was appropriate for them to call me by my first name for the same reason most parents don't encourage their children to do that. So we decided to be creative. It took a while, but we eventually adopted names that work for us.

The elder son calls me Popper, and the younger calls me Writer. The name of Popper is an affectionate term that refers to my paternal role in his life. But the strong-willed younger son wanted to come up with his own name for me. He chose Writer, because that is what he sees me doing at nights in my study at home.

The particular name is not as important as the process of allowing the children to decide how to refer to this man who has taken on an intimate role of leadership in their lives. As long as it was endearing, I didn't really care what they chose. But there was no clear guide for this. Our invented names work just fine, largely because the boys played a part in determining what they would be. These names have stuck. I'm sure that at my funeral they will still be calling me Popper and Writer, and that pleases me a great deal.

Who Takes Care of Mom?

Every family looks for a sense of balance, and that typically means adjusting to its problems by developing some dysfunctional patterns of behavior. When blending a stepfather into a family, the dysfunctions of both prior family systems soon come to light. For example, it's not unusual to discover that he's in emotional competition with his wife's oldest son. This was never a dramatic dynamic in our family, but we do see some form of it now and then.

While Dawne was a single mother, her older son took on the role of providing her emotional support. She neither elicited this nor played into it. But there was just something in him, even as a young boy, that needed to assure his mother was okay. Sometimes this manifested itself in harmless activities like frequent offers for foot rubs. At other times it was clear that he was too anxious about his mother's well-being. He was old enough to witness the breakup of Dawne's prior marriage to his father, and this embedded in him a sense of the fragility of his own well-being.

Before we were married, we assumed that her older son would perceive me as a threat to his perception of himself as his mother's primary companion. But it didn't work out that way. To the contrary, he soon became anxious to ensure that our marriage was going well. Early in our marriage he used to ask a lot of questions about the permanence of our relationship. Five years later, he is happy that his mother is happy, and he just wants things to stay on an even keel. It is still hard on him to hear Dawne and me arguing about even small matters because he's such an advocate for our marriage. This is clearly better for him than feeling like he has to be the caregiver for his mother, but she and I still have to assure him of the security of our relationship in order to free him to think just about the issues of being a typical teenager.

Dawne doesn't need anyone to take care of her. She is strong, gifted, hardworking, tenacious in her capacity to get what she wants, and a fierce mother bear. But she does need the care that comes only from being securely loved by a partner. That's the tricky part for single mothers when they remarry. They have the burden of assuring their children that this new man can handle the responsibility.

This has become one of the bonds between the older son and me. While I dearly love and enjoy both of the boys, I have bonded in different ways to them. Since I grew up as a younger son, I have immediate empathy for the baby of our family. I naturally get this kid, adore his passion, and take great delight in seeing how his impishness can make Dawne smile. I remember being able to create that exact same smile for my mother. Our older son also brings great joy to his mother, but he and I share the common concern of making sure that everything is okay. Especially with her. He's fine with letting me fill the role and is clear that I'm in the best position to do that. And yet, he watches. That makes me love him all the more because I have a sense that he understands my own calling.

The Ex

There are lots of novels and popular media images that depict healthy relationships between ex-spouses. Neither Dawne nor I have that experience. We both struggle with these strained relationships, and the strain shows up especially around issues involving the boys.

They typically spend Friday nights at their father's house. We understand the importance of this for the boys' development, and believe that their father loves his sons. But he has his own way of relating to them, which is very different from our way. His house is filled with ping–pong and pool tables, video games, and various toys lying around on the floor. The boys rightly love their Dad, and certainly have a good time with him. Gratefully, they are also happy to come home the following evening. We used to find them sluggish or moody for a day as they transitioned back home. But after five years of this, they seem to have developed a sense of rhythm to their week.

Although he and Dawne have a strained relationship, it's at least functional. He and I have no relationship at all. It is still very awkward when we bump into each other at youth baseball games and school events. The boys are aware of these tensions, and we struggle to make sure they are not caught in the middle of them. But it still happens.

For example, one Christmas the boys' father bought them an electronic game we had long decided they should not have. The e-mails flew back and forth as my wife protested, and he protested her protests. In the end, the best we could do was to surrender to the reality. We explained again to the boys why we would not have the game in our house, but we didn't want them to feel guilty for enjoying it in his house. That makes sense to adults, but it's hard for children to get their heads around it. They complained about being stuck in their parents' argument, which clearly they were.

This is another illustration of why it is best for children to be raised in a home where their mother and father still love each other, stay married, and are able to create a single family culture for them. As much as Dawne and I love each other and are completely devoted to our family, we believe this is not the best way to raise children. It's an accommodation for the failure of prior marriages. But family life these days is often messy. So like many others we cope the best way we can, believing that love, hard work, and a whole lot of grace can cover our limitations.

Root Experiences

Dawne and I believe it is very important to have family adventures. Sometimes this means loading the family up on a plane and heading out for an expensive vacation. More often it just means touch football in the park on a Sunday afternoon, playing a lawn game in the backyard, or even having family business meetings where everyone has to wear a funny hat while we talk our way through the calendar of activities for the month ahead.

These are what I call root experiences. Essentially they are ways of creating memories from which the boys can continue to draw reassuring affirmations of the health of their family. We want them to one day sit around their own family table and tell stories about the wonderful things they did as children. All families need these experiences, but it is particularly important for the parents of a blended family to create these good memories. Our children need to believe that the family is more than just blended. It is a daily expression of what love means.

Not all root experiences are comfortable, and some good memories come out of hard times. Two years ago we had to deal with significant medical issues in both of our boys' lives. Our older son was diagnosed with scoliosis a few months before the younger one contracted type 1 diabetes. This created major obstacles for the boys and deep grief for us. We are still not at the point of finding the redemption of these problems, but it has focused us on what is important as a family. Dawne and I share the management of their medical and therapeutic treatments. Although she is the primary caregiver, it is important that the boys see us responding to their problems as a team. Often one of us is dealing with one set of medical issues, like insurance, while the other is handling doctors and physical therapists. We take turns handling glucose readings at 3:00 a.m., adjustments to a back brace, and frequent trips to physicians. At no point in any of this do I act differently than I would have if the boys were my biological sons. That's been a good thing for all four of us. It helps us to keep faith in the family we have.

We do not want our boys to grow up saying they came from a broken home. Of course, we have experienced brokenness. But not necessarily more than any other family. We want the boys to have as normal an experience of growing up as possible, and that means that we never allow the issues of divorce and remarriage to define us. We don't ignore those issues, but we also take the initiative to create plenty of normal experiences, and we respond to the crises of life like any loving family would.

It is also important that Dawne and I have root experiences as a couple without the boys. As even they realize, the most important thing we can do for them is to maintain a healthy, loving marriage. So at least once a year we schedule a vacation for the two of us, which we distinguish from a family trip. Also, a blessing of the boys spending Friday nights with their father is that it leaves us with a built-in date night every week. We became a blended family because Dawne and I fell in love with each other. So, clearly I don't want my devotion to being a good stepfather get in the way of my devotion to being a good husband. But it's actually more complicated than that.

I used to think of our marriage at the core of the family and the children as the next concentric ring. Work and everything else were just more rings. The way it actually works is that the circling rings collapse into each other all the time. Even when we are alone on a couple's vacation, we spend an incredible amount of time talking about the boys. Because we want to. And when I am sitting next to my wife on the bleachers at a youth baseball game, I find a quiet, deep pleasure. I know her better because I know these two boys who cannot be pulled from her heart to another circle.

Spirituality

It is impossible to describe how important our faith has been to us as we embarked on creating our new family. We quickly knew that we were in way over our heads, and so we prayed constantly for wisdom and courage. But we neither expected nor received any extraterrestrial help with the hard issues. Instead we received the promise of Scripture and the creeds that consistently affirms we're not alone. That has been enough.

At the time of writing, I served as senior pastor of a Presbyterian congregation and a tenured professor at a nearby seminary. While the seminary had no expectations of Dawne, early in our marriage she had to adjust to being the pastor's wife. And our boys learned how to handle the visibility of being preacher's kids. I served the same congregation that witnessed my divorce, my single years, and my remarriage. Visibility is just the norm in our family. Once everyone got used to that, it hasn't been particularly burdensome. However, the boys often chafed at *having to* go to Sunday school and youth group. I doubt we would be as demanding about this if I were not the pastor.

The much harder spiritual issues have been internal to our family. When we're exhausted from our boys' medical problems, when their biological father decides to be a pain in the neck just to let us know he can, or when Dawne cannot bear to hear me whine one more time that I'm still a outsider at home, it helps that we know how to pray. In prayer we ask for the vision to see that God is with us.

As this Creator once shoved aside the dark chaos to make room for light and beauty, so can our little and often chaotic family find hope. The hope isn't that we will magically be transformed into the Brady Bunch. We hope just that the Spirit of God will make us a bit more careful with each other. If we can treat everyone in the family as a living testimony to the presence of God, the vast majority of our issues would evaporate before they could do much damage.

Far more important, as we pay attention to the grace we have received from God, we are more attentive to the grace we find in each other. And any family held together by grace has every reason to be hopeful.

10

What Are Fathers For?[1]

ANTHONY B. ROBINSON

What are fathers for? Are fathers indispensable or dispensable? What is it exactly that fathers do, or that they are supposed to do? Like so many things, these questions are prompted by social changes that are both positive and negative. On the plus side, gender roles are less restrictive or prescribed than was the case a generation or two ago. It is not so clear as it once was that women do this and men do that. The negative side of things is that too many fathers are simply missing in action. Perhaps they never married the woman who gave birth to their child or children, and have then disappeared altogether. Or maybe they have only a minor role as a result of divorce or custody battles. For too many children, life is *Life Without Father*, the title of a recent book that studied and enumerated the negative consequences of this development.

When we were expecting our first child, we lived in Hilo, Hawaii, a small town on the windward side of the island of Hawaii, also known as "the Big Island." Across the street lived Miss Katherine Beveridge, a regal yet warm and lively octogenarian. Katherine's father had captained whaling ships, and she came to Hawaii aboard one around the turn of the last century. She had lived her entire life there in Hilo, teaching elementary school. Though she had never had children of her own, she had taught hundreds of children all over the island and knew as much about kids and parents as anyone I've ever known. By the time we got to know her, Katherine was at that stage of life where she was shrinking in size but still large, even growing, in stature.

As my wife's pregnancy advanced I must have felt some anxiety about fatherhood because one day I wondered aloud to Katherine about how I would do as a parent and as a father. She laughed a bit and said, "You'll do fine, just trust yourself." She saw that what I needed was less a matter of instruction and more a dose of reassurance. There is no real or adequate instruction for the business of being a father. It's too big, too variable, and too open ended. But for all those reasons we do need reassurance and we need trust.

What do fathers do? Are fathers providers, disciplinarians, supporters, teachers, guides, lawgivers, defenders, coaches, or confidants—all of the above or none of the above? I think I have played all those roles for my own children, two sons and a daughter, though with varying degrees of success. Nevertheless, I am not sure any one of the list, nor the entire list taken together, answers the question, what are fathers for? The real answer seems so obvious as to be hidden in plain sight. Fathers are part of the primal human community that engages in the most basic and most complex of tasks: raising the next generation. The oft-cited proverb "It takes a whole village to raise a child" starts with the very first village of two different people. It is probably no accident that this proverb became popular about the time life without father was becoming much more common.

If it is true that parents must strive for a balance between two kinds of love (accepting love and transforming love), then a father and a mother may embody these two kinds of love and in doing so balance one another. If accepting love affirms the being of a child and lets them be, then transforming love seeks their well-being and prods their growth. The interesting and probably controversial question is whether a father's (or a mother's) love is necessarily one of these two loves? In other words, does a mother's love tend to be the accepting love, while the father's love is the transformative complement, or vice versa? And if each kind of love can be assigned to one parent, is that nature's proper order or society's preferred construction? Surely, the two loves can and do dwell in one person. Surely too there are countless incidences when the father's love is more of the accepting variety and the mother's love more of the transforming.

These are questions to which I have no answer. What I do have, however, is this observation: It is the father's blessing that is more often than not the one that is sought and in some sense earned as opposed to given freely. If true, this suggests that more often it is the father who holds or conveys the transforming love. In my own life, and in many others, I have heard stories of the father's blessing being given; not nearly so often, rarely in fact, have I heard similar stories of the giving of the mother's blessing. This may be because of the nature of childbirth and nurture. Mothers and children are bound together at the beginning while fathers are at an inevitable distance. Or it may be because, whether by nature or nurture, fathers tend to more often be the embodiment of the transforming love while mothers embody an accepting love.

I certainly remember how long I waited before receiving a blessing from my own father, who had Alzheimer's disease. During his last three years he lived in a small facility with twenty others in various stages of the disease. Often I visited him alone, simply because it was harder for my wife to get away from work. However, the summer before he died, we were both there for a visit. The three of us were walking together arm in arm, my wife and I on either side of him. We moved at his slow pace across the dining room toward the door, which opened to an enclosed garden. By this time my dad seldom said much that made sense to us. Even his words had become difficult to understand, his speech often slurred. As we crossed the dining room his slippered shuffle drew to a halt. Bent over, he looked up at me and clear as a bell said, "You are a good man." Then he resumed his shuffle toward the door. My wife said, "Did you hear that?" She did not mean, "Did you hear the words he said?" She meant, "Did you hear, really hear, what he was saying to you?" It was my father's blessing. Three months later, he died.

Even though I have heard such stories of a father's blessing many times as a pastor, my own experience of it came as if I had never heard a one. It was as unexpected and as pleasing a gift as a rainbow. But almost all the stories of such blessings seem to be stories of the father's, not the mother's, blessing. The mother's blessing seems to have ben imparted long ago, in the womb, and to have required no conferral. Yes, clearly there are many exceptions to this as a pattern, but the pattern itself stands. In this sense, it is the father's love that is more of the growth-prodding and demanding, while a mother's is more of the accepting and letting be.

But this exploration of the double face of love, or the two loves of parents, can be taken a step further. So often in life truth lies in holding the tension of competing truths, in holding "the tension of polarity," as

Kierkegaard put it. The tension between accepting love and transforming love should never be resolved in favor or one pole or the other. Both poles are absolutely necessary. One does not solve or resolve such polarities. One lives with them, balancing and managing them. Having two parents is like having both ends of a seesaw occupied. This can be tough. I say, time to let go, while my wife says, time to hold on. Usually we're both right, and both are true. Wisdom lies in finding the course between. Being a father is being part of this duo and duet, this dance, and holding down your side of the seesaw of things. Left to our own devices and desires, many of us would tilt out of balance. My hat is off to those who manage the daunting job of raising kids as single parents, but I don't envy them. Two parents in it together is a good idea whenever possible. We all need other people who are close enough to the situation and close enough to us to give us an honest reality check, to keep us balanced even as we balance the other.

The trick in all the various roles parents play is doing it without overdoing it. The Taoist philosopher Lao-tzu once counseled the emperor "to govern as you fry a small fish—lightly." Children are small fish, and at least for a time, parents loom as large as emperors. Our touch as parents and as fathers needs to be light but firm; doing enough but not overdoing it. Providing but not providing everything, protecting without hovering, nurturing without stifling, teaching without being heavy handed.

Because so much of being parents seems to be about doing but not overdoing, I return to the obvious but lately problematic point about what fathers are for. Being a parent is not a solo act. Neither fathers nor mothers have a child, so far, by themselves. The seesaw nature of parenthood is a good reason for two parents to be involved and engaged, balancing one another and thus raising reasonably balanced children. What are fathers for? The answer is hidden in plain sight. We are an essential part of the parental package, part of the first and primary human community our children know.

11

The Sweet Ironies of Fatherhood

MICHAEL L. LINDVALL

The Unhelpful Helpfulness of Scripture

Frankly, Christian Scripture is only oddly and ironically helpful to men who would be good fathers. The most famous fathers in the Bible appear in the last thirty-nine chapters of the Book of Genesis. The great family saga of that book, with its three fathers, the patriarchs Abraham, Isaac and Jacob, tells of a multigenerational clan that would surely be named dysfunctional by any modern family therapist.

Abraham is quite ready to send his firstborn, Ishmael, and Ishmael's mother, Abraham's servant, to die in the desert so that Abraham can dote on Isaac, the child of his marriage, a favorite he is nevertheless prepared to slay if God demands it. This Isaac survives his father only to favor one of his twin sons, the two of whom fall into a malicious rivalry. The younger, named heir only through his deception, fathers twelve sons, eleven of whom conspire to murder the favorite. There are scant models in the first book of the Bible for the man who would be a loving and nurturing father! The rest of Hebrew Scripture presents us with but few fathers, none of them exemplars either. Jesse is dismissive of his youngest son, David. David and his reign may have become a theological archetype, but the great king was hardly the ideal family man.

Nevertheless, the Older Testament offers a light to fathers in at least two specific ways. First, it functions rather as a cautionary tale: this is how you *don't* do it. Favoritism, anger, jealousy, and self-seeking will bear their bitter fruits, even in God's family. But more important, the wild families of Hebrew Scripture, especially the protofamily of Genesis, are narrative enactments of the great truth that God's graceful purposes can bring great good out of even the most messed-up family. Joseph speaks this verity after rising to power in Egypt and revealing his identity to the brothers who had once sought his death and have now come to Egypt for the famine relief that he is in a position to offer: "You meant evil against me; God meant it for good."

As a father, I find great comfort and hope in this, a providential dynamic I trust to be true in my imperfect family as well as in Abraham's, namely, that as he did with Jacob, God can work through my foibles and in spite of my fatherly weaknesses to nurture blessing in and for my children. That is to say, neither their mother nor I are on our own in this daunting parenting enterprise. I suppose this is why I pray for my three children every night. I know I am not fully the father they need and never can be, but God is.

The Newer Testament is centered on two men especially, Jesus and Paul, neither of whom were fathers. Paul has a fatherly relationship with Timothy, but he did not raise the young man even though he nurtures his protégé in the faith in an exemplary manner. For obvious reasons, tradition never names Jesus Father. He is Teacher, Messiah, Lord, and Savior; later, Brother, but never Father, a theological name the Gospels reserve for God-in-God's-self, the God to whom Jesus prays and names as such. Yet it is in Jesus, never named Father, that this father finds the most helpful succor in my struggle to be a good father to my children. We will come back to Jesus and fatherhood at the end of this essay.

This Father

I have three adult children. All three are generally happy. All three go to church. All three seem to like to be with their mother and me. It occurred to me that as a father invited to write an essay on fatherhood, I might ask my children about the subject. So during a recent family vacation, I sat each one of them down separately and interviewed them on the subject of fatherhood in general and me as a father specifically. I asked them to be candid as they could and to avoid clichés like "You were always there for us." I learned a few things that I mixed with my memories of my own father's fathering, plus my ongoing experience of being a father. I then set these interview observations, memories and experiences in the context of the Christian convictions that I would have shape my life.

The Road Is the Teacher

You learn to ride a bicycle by riding a bicycle. Instruction that notes the placement and function of pedals, brakes, and shift controls is most helpful, but the mere knowing of such things will not enable you to ride a bike. You simply have to do it. You have to throw a leg over the saddle and go. You will be wobbly at first; you may run into things; you may fall over. But it's the only way. As with bicycle riding, life's great teacher is the living of life itself. That is to say, the road is the teacher.

The Victorian novelist Edward Bulwer-Lytton said that "Life is like learning to play the violin and giving your first concert at the same time." So too fatherhood. There is no school to prepare you to be a father save your own memories of your father's fathering, and he was a man who had no more training in fatherhood than you. A great many things in life are learned only in the stubborn, faithful, and concrete *doing* of them. They are generally the things that matter most. Faith is perhaps the best example. Doctrine can be taught; theology can be read; the faithful lives of others are exemplars, but one comes to faith by doing faith: worshiping, praying, confessing, doing justice and mercy, and believing even when you barely believe.

This same principle applies to fatherhood in two ways. First, I learn to be a father mostly by actually being a father. Such learning requires that I watch my fathering most closely. I must observe my actions and inactions. I am called to be confessionally critical of myself as a father, noting and admitting my laziness, my excuses, my too-quick anger, my selfishness, pride in my children that so easily edges into pride in myself. I must look for successes in fathering as well: what gives my children joy and confidence, what gives me joy and confidence in fathering. Day by day, week by week, year by year, my fathering teaches me to be a father, but only if I have the courage and honesty to learn from the doing of it.

Second, as I learn to be a father in the act of fathering, my children must learn to be men and women of faith, compassion, purpose, and integrity in the doing of just those things. This implies two things: I must first walk those roads with them, side by side, and then, in time, I must release my hand from theirs and let them take to the road alone. If I long for them to be adults who pray, I must pray with them as children. In my interviews with them, all three of my children remembered, quite independently, that I had regularly prayed with them as children. If I wish them to be adults who treasure wisdom, I must read with them and to them, and they must see me reading for myself. All three spoke of being read to, well after they had learned to read themselves. If I desire my children to grow into compassionate adults, I must work at compassion with them as children, traveling with them on a mission trip to Maine, pounding nails beside them at a Habitat for Humanity build. In our interviews, they all remembered such things much more sharply than I.

Then I must remember that the road will be their teacher as well, and if they are to learn from it, they must eventually take to it without me. It's not just the letting go that's hard; it's not just the erosion of parental control that surfaces in the teen years; it's not just watching them make mistakes in their twenties. Hardest of all is to trust them and to trust that God is with them in the false turns and bad choices—turns and choices that will bring them pain and disappointment, but pain and disappointment that will teach them what they cannot learn from me. They are not me; nor are they my handiwork, no mere reflections of my ability as a father or worth as a man. Just as the road has been my teacher, the road is and will be their teacher. I trust that God is in the road.

Hypocrisy Radar

Children have abilities that adults do not. My two-year-old granddaughter can touch her toes to her forehead; I cannot. Children are also equipped with the uncanny ability to detect the slightest variation between what adults say and what they do. I call this "hypocrisy radar." Children, especially when they are teenagers, will often loudly announce the detection of such inconsistency in adults (their parents in particular) with statements prefaced by, "But you *said!*" But more worrisome than such protestations, children will often observe inconsistency, say nothing, and remember . . . for a very long time.

Their hypocrisy radar presents me as a father with two challenges. The first, of course, is to aim for the greatest integrity I might achieve between what I say and what I do. This is very difficult, nearly impossible; for one of the skills adults keenly posses that children do not is the ability to rationalize, to subtly excuse the inconsistency between adult word and adult action with reasonable-sounding pleas of "practical considerations and common sense." This is sharply true for Christians who are bound by a word that demands actions that are nearly, if not altogether, impossible to carry out fully. When I've asked teenagers or adult children of faithful parents, teenagers and adult children who do not go to church or much believe anymore, why they have not followed their parents in the faith, the commonest answer I have heard is that of perceived inconsistency between what their parents and their church believed and what both actually did.

The second challenge my children's hypocrisy radar presents me is that I honestly confess, to them and to God, the inconsistent correspondence between what God demands of me, indeed what I would ask of myself, and what I actually do. This is quite different from rationalizing. Rather, it is to enter into the discipline of confession and grace, a dialectic (if the grace not be cheap) that would pull me toward an ever more perfect integrity between word and deed. As I father, I do this by tutoring them (by word and deed), not in the rationalization that I am so good at, but rather in the confession I find so difficult.

The Myth of Quality Time

I have heard more than a few busy fathers profess their belief that if they make their meager time with their children "quality time," they are fulfilling their fatherly duties and meeting their children's needs. I suppose "quality time" means time in which you do something intense, perhaps engaging in some activity organized in advance, one that needs to be planned and paid for.

My experience and my children's memories would suggest otherwise. It is so often the unplanned and outwardly uneventful time spent with children that proves to be most precious and affecting. In my conversations with my children, all spoke of how important it was for a father to be present with children in the routine of life, sharing in daily chores and mundane pleasures—watering geraniums and making evening popcorn the old-fashioned way. They all mentioned our family's dogged insistence on sitting down to dinner together every night—no eating alone or late-afternoon grazing; rather dinner at the table together, even if you don't want to talk, even if you're not hungry. The demanding truth is that there is no substitute for time given a child in substantial quantity. "Quality time" is mostly a cop-out.

A Fenced-In Back Yard

In our summer vacation interviews, all three of my children reflected on the delicate balance between limits and freedom that they experienced growing up. It seems the backyard was big enough to allow some freedom to explore . . . but there was (make no mistake) a fence around that yard, and they were glad it was there. At least that's what they say now. This dialectic between freedom and boundaries is akin to that of law and grace in Scripture and theology. Now that my children are largely grown and looking back, they value what they recall as a well-tuned balance. When they were younger, they seemed to long only for grace. Of course, the hidden truth (never admitted by any self-respecting child) is that they secretly wanted some law as well, even then. For if our law was fair, it suggested that we cared for them and that we loved them. Rules also gave them a reason ("my parents are *so* strict") that they could offer to their peers for not doing something they really didn't want to do anyway.

For instance, one rule in the Lindvall household was that if you lived under our roof and ate from our table, you went to church. You could choose Sunday school or worship, but we all went to church. You didn't have to like it; you could wear most anything you wanted, you were free to choose to attend the youth group or not, you could dodge coffee hour, but on Sunday morning everybody in the family went to church. At the time they complained, intermittently and often loudly. Now they all recall it fondly as a formative discipline. "Home," my daughter said, "made me confident." She didn't mean only the love; she meant the rules too.

In time they will open the gate and leave the fenced-in backyard, of course. That moment seems to come later and more ambiguously today than it once did. College graduates move back home in great number; jobs and health insurance are scarce; marriage is something you do in your thirties. Adolescence has been effectively protracted, often creating a near-decade of almost-adulthood, a time when the parental dance of law and grace grows clumsy. Does a twenty-three-year-old living at home need a curfew?

But in time, they all do open the gate and leave the backyard. What they knew there in the yard, both the law and the grace, will guide them in the world on the other side of the gate. Calvin famously insisted on three uses of the law, theologically speaking. First, the law shows us our shortcomings. Second, the law maintains good order—in family, church, and civil community. And third, even though God's grace is the dominant theme in the shaping of Christian life, the law functions as a guide to the living of obedient lives shaped by Spirit. So when they come to leave the backyard, it's not only grace they take with them but the light burden and good gift of law as well.

Jesus as Father

I remember the day a lifelong friend, a man about my age and the father of four, sat down in a living room chair after a long day of fatherhood and opined that "being a father means that you never get to do what you want to do when you want to do it ever again." A hyperbole of course, but one pointing emphatically at a fundamental veracity. Fatherhood means yielding of self.

When I counsel couples before their weddings, I tell them that getting married will change their lives, but not nearly as much as becoming parents will, should that lie before them. Fatherhood (one would hope as much as motherhood) implies a radical reorientation of a man's universe. The center of your personal cosmos suddenly becomes that beloved little bundle of loud noises and foul smells that is your child. By the grace of God, this leads, one hopes and fears, to an elemental dethronement of self. Our natural proclivity is to construct a personal solar system with ourselves set at the center, perched on the throne as it were, with others revolving about us like planets around a sun. Suddenly, this picture is redrawn by great love. Marriage itself would teach us the same lesson of course, but hardly with the relentlessness of fatherhood. "Marriage," Luther said, "is a school for the soul." The man had children as well as a wife, and surely had both in mind. The lesson the school teaches is that other human beings, their hopes and fears, their blessing and safely, matter at least as much as your own. You are not, after all, the center of the universe.

As I noted early in this essay, neither Scripture nor tradition name Jesus father. Nevertheless, his way is the way toward ideal fatherhood. At the heart of the love and life of Jesus was his self-yielding and abiding concern for the lives of others, even at the cost of his own life. He taught this self-yielding. He lived this self-yielding. He died for this self-yielding. He rose to empower us to love and live in some imitation of this self-yielding. In his radical willingness to live for the other, Jesus is the archetype, the *telos*, the goal of ideal fatherhood. For real fatherhood, if it brings anything, brings a man to yield self for the love of another. "Being a father means that you never get to do what you want to do when you want to do it ever again."

But the rest of the story is that my friend has found unimaginable joy in his fatherhood, reveling in children no more perfect than mine or any. For beyond a father's yielding of self there lies a life more abundant than any lived merely for self. In the giving is the receiving. In the losing is the finding. In yielding is life.

Bibliography

Barnes, M. Craig. *Yearning: Living between How It Is and How It Ought to Be*. Downers Grove, IL: InterVarsity, 1991.

Chesterton, G. K. *All Things Considered*. New York: Lane, 1909.

Clapp, Rodney. *Families at the Crossroads: Beyond Traditional & Modern Options*. Downers Grove, IL: InterVarsity, 1993.

Clark, William A., SJ. "Mystery." In *An Introductory Dictionary of Theology and Religious Studies*, edited by Orlando O. Espín and James B. Nickoloff, 923. Collegeville, MN: Liturgical, 2007.

Cole, Allan Hugh, Jr. *Be Not Anxious: Pastoral Care of Disquieted Souls*. Grand Rapids: Eerdmans, 2008.

Daly, Mary. *Beyond God the Father: Toward a Philosophy of Women's Liberation*. Boston: Beacon, 1985.

Jung, C. G. *Psychological Reflections: An Anthology of the Writings of C. G. Jung*. Edited by Jolande Jacoby. New York: Harper, 1961.

Robinson, Anthony B. *Common Grace: How to Be a Person and Other Spiritual Matters*. Seattle: Sasquatch, 2006.

Seneca, Lucius Annaeus. "On the Shortness of Life." In *Moral Essays*, vol. 2. Translated by John W. Basore, 341. Rev. ed. Loeb Classical Library 254. Cambridge: Harvard University Press, 1932.